FRESH WATER FISH DISEASE IN UTTARAKHAND

RAKESH VERMA

PRIYANKA SHARMA

Woven Words Publishers OPC Pvt. Ltd.

Registered Office:

Vill: Raipur, P.O: Raipur Paschimbar,

Dist: Purba Midnapore, Pin: 721401,

West Bengal, India.

Branch Office (Operations): Hyderabad

www.wovenwordspublishers.com

Email: publish@wovenwordspublishers.com

First published by Woven Words Publishers OPC Pvt. Ltd., 2021

Price: Rs. 300/-

IMPRINT: WOVEN WORDS ACADEMIC

ISBN 13: 978-93-91209-03-2
ISBN 10: 93-91209-03-3

CONTENT

PREFACE

This comprehensive part of the manuscript covers the major freshwater fish diseases in the state of Uttarakhand. This book covers various frequently occurring diseases in fishes, as bacterial, fungal, and viral diseases are very common in fishes and affect various parts of the fish body. Fins, gills, eyes, the whole body, the ventral surface of the body, the abdomen region, and the mouth region are the various body parts which get affected frequently and commonly in freshwater fishes. Although diseases are very rare in freshwater conditions, some common and frequently occurring diseases, especially in the freshwater of the Himalayan region of Uttarakhand State, are being focused here. It is actually a research report from Uttarakhand on the given topic, after an extensive literature survey by the authors and personal field experience of the authors. This book is aimed at providing detailed scientific information on the fish disease for university students, parasitologists, environmental toxicologists, and various research scholars. This research will be helpful to future scientific study in this field to establish the ecological relationship between fish disease and its ecosystem, which will lead to sustainable ecosystem development. The freshwater fisheries of the state will also benefit from this review on fish diseases.

Rakesh Verma

Priyanka Sharma

ACKNOWLEDGEMENTS

Writing a recharge report is nearly often the last stage in any research and one of the most difficult aspects of any researcher's job. After considerable writing, a thank-you note appears to be an essential element of every study project. Initially, authors express gratitude to the almighty God for providing them with the chance to work and write. It would be impossible to complete the work on time without the assistance of family members. Our sincere appreciation to the renowned institution's head, the department's head, and department faculty members for their unwavering support, encouragement, inspiration, and aid, as well as helpful ideas. The concluding recognition to various research scholars for their enormous contribution to this work is unforgettable.

Rakesh Verma

Priyanka Sharma

ABSTRACT

This study focuses on various fish diseases, particularly in the Himalayan area of Uttarakhand State's fresh water conditions. It is, in fact, a study paper based on a thorough literature review and personal field experience in Uttarakhand on the subject, since bacterial, fungal, and viral illnesses are all too frequent in fish. Fins, gills, eyes, the entire body, the ventral side of the body, the abdominal area, and the mouth region are some of the body parts that are affected by fish sickness. The study's major goals were to learn more about freshwater fish illness and to establish a link between the host and the pathogen in the environment.

This book aims to present a detailed review of fish diseases in the Himalayan area of Uttarakhand State's fresh water conditions. The topic is wide as disease occur in freshwater and marine aquacultures as well as in wild fish. This manuscript is intended to provide thorough scientific information about the fish disease to a variety of researchers, as well as to aid future scientific research in the subject. This study will aid in determining the ecological link between fish disease and ecosystem development, which will lead to long-term ecosystem growth. This study will also be helpful for environmental toxicologists and parasitologists to establish an ecological relationship between fish disease and its ecosystem.

This study is mainly divided into three sections, Disease Condition (or to know the name of the disease), Symptoms (that occur during the disease condition), and Pathogens Involvement. Four types of bacterial disease, three types of fungal diseases, and two types of viral disease are discussed in this study.

In this review investigation. four different forms of bacterial diseases were discussed. Fin and Tail rot Disease was caused by *Aeromonas salmonici,* and the main signs and symptoms include; erosions, discolorations and disintegration of fin and tail. The main symptoms of Dropsy, caused by *Pseudomonas punctata*, were haemorrhagic lesions on skin, fins, tail. Columnaris Disease, caused by *Chondroccus columnaris*, and the main symptoms were haemorrhagic and ulcerative lesions on fins, head, back, which may look yellow to orange. *Aeromonas liquifaciens* causes eye disease with the following symptoms; Cataract of eyes that affect the cornea, and the eyeball gets putrefied.

Three main types of fungal disease were also noticed in this review study. Saprolegniasis, caused by *Saprolegnia parasitica*, and the main symptoms were; Fish become weak, ulceration of skin with haemorrhages, cotton wool growth on ulcers with grey patches. Branchiomycosis (Gill rot disease), caused by *Branchiomyces demigrans,* and the main symptoms were; Fish become lethargic, redness of gills, which later become greyish-white, necrosis of gill filaments. Icthyophonus Disease (Swinging Disease), caused by *Icthyophonus hoferi*, and the primary symptoms involved; swinging movement of fish.

This review study also discussed main types of viral disease. The main symptoms of Carp spring viremia (CSV), caused by *Rhabdovirus carpio,* were lethargy, staying towards tank bottom, and awkward swimming. Another viral disease caused by Rhabdovirus is Viral Haemorrhagic septicemia virus (VHSV), having symptoms like anaemia, pale discolouration of gill, swelling of eyes and belly, odema of muscles, inflammation of intestine, and anus being protruded.

GENERAL INTRODUCTION

This study is about the various fish diseases especially on the fresh water condition of Himalayan region, Uttarakhand State. It is actually a research report after extensive literature survey and personal field experience from the Uttarakhand on the given topic, as bacterial, fungal, and viral diseases are very common in fishes. Fish disease affect various parts of the fish body, such as Fins, gills, eyes, the whole body, the ventral surface of the body, the abdomen region, and the mouth region are the various body parts. Main objectives of the study were to know the freshwater fish disease and to establish environmental relationship between host pathogen. This manuscript is aimed to provide detail scientific information on the fish disease for the various researchers and will also be helpful for the future scientific study in this field. This research will be helpful to establish the ecological relationship between fish disease and its ecosystem which lead to sustainable ecosystem development. This study will also be helpful for environmental toxicologists, parasitologists to establish ecological relationship between fish disease and its ecosystem

Fisheries play an important role in food security and livelihood in developing countries, and also serve as a source of income revenue for social development (FAO, 2016). Fishes not only play an important role in the demand for food for humans, but they have also emerged as major model organisms for biomedical research. Food enhanced in nutritional level is in high demand worldwide, in both developing and emerging countries (Sen and Mandal, 2018). Among all fishes, freshwater fishes are an important source of protein for people in many countries (Hussain et al., 2011; Rubbani et al., 2011). In India, fishing is the most progressive and growing sector. Freshwater fish also play a great role in biological research in today's life (Ch. Sarojnalini and Abdul Hei, 2019). Recently, the sector has attracted great attention and it is growing rapidly through the development of aquaculture (Kubecka et al., 2016). New technological advances and an increased demand for fish as a source of animal protein are the main reasons for the industry's growth.

Fish, like other animals, are susceptible to a variety of diseases. Pathogens and parasites are found in every fish. Aquaculture diseases are one of the main constraints to the fishing sector, which harms fish farmers' livelihoods, results in job losses, lower income, and decreased food security. According to studies, diseases, which are more severe in developing countries, account for about half of the production losses. This is due to the fact that 90% of the aquaculture firms are located in underdeveloped countries. Disease-related revenue losses reach as high as $6 billion each year. According to Sniezko (1974), the disease is caused by a complex interaction between the host, pathogen and the environment. The majority of parasitic, fungal, and bacterial pathogens are not parasitic. These pathogens are more vulnerable to changes in the environment. If pathogens thrive in the environment, a saprophytic relationship between the host and the pathogen will develop. Environmental stress is a major constraint on the increased occurrence of these infections (Mishra, et. al., 2017).

However, disease in fish, on the other hand, is not understood well. What is known about fish disease often relates to freshwater fish, and more recently, to farmed fish. Disease is a major factor in fish mortality, especially in young fishes. Fish that can reduce the impact of diseases and parasites by behavioral or biochemical means have a competitive reproductive advantage. Low-grade infections become lethal diseases as a result of interactions between factors. Things that induce stress, such as natural droughts, pollution, or predators, can trigger a disease outbreak in particular. When diseases and parasites carried by introduced species infect native species, disease can become a major issue. To avoid losses in aquaculture due to infectious diseases, it is vital to address each health constraint based on scientifically proven and recommended as well as locally applicable ways.

The demand for epidemiological measures to keep aquatic animal health safe is driven by challenges in aquaculture due to environmental changes such as climate change, limited water sources, and growth (Peeler and Taylor, 2011). As "prevention is better than treatment," it is advisable to focus on preventing the occurrence of disease rather than treating it (Romero et al., 2012). The best approaches to controlling infectious diseases in fish are improved management practices, movement restrictions, genetically resistant stock, dietary supplements, nonspecific immune-stimulants, vaccines, probiotics, prebiotics, medicinal plant products, water disinfection, biological control, antimicrobial compounds, water disinfection, and movement control (Kumar et al., 2016).

In India and many other nations around the world, disease is one of the biggest constraints to aquaculture and a limiting factor for economic and socio-economic development (Bagum et al., 2013; Mohan and Bhatta, 2002; Sahoo et al., 2013). Some diseases have caused serious damage, not only to the livelihoods of fish farmers, but also to the future development of the industry. Many diseases affecting modern aquaculture are the result of cultural practices being intensified without a basic understanding of the intricate balance between host, pathogen and environment (Bondad et al., 2005; Subasinghe et al., 2001). The rise of aquaculture production in India, particularly in intensive and semi-intensive methods, has been accompanied by an increase in fish and shellfish due to high stocking densities and stress circumstances that favour the emergence and spread of infectious illnesses (Mishra et al. 2017).

Diseases in shrimp culture have resulted in a total loss of one billion dollars (Mishra et al., 2017). The more frequent occurrence of bacterial, fungal, and viral infections has occurred due to the vertical growth of fish culture with varied species and higher stocking density, often resulting in higher morbidity or mass mortalities and reduced productivity. Rural resource poor farmers with little or no knowledge of fish health management and skills to prevent and control disease outbreaks are the biggest sufferers, incurring huge economic loss (Bagum et al., 2013). The emergence of disease is thought to be the outcome of a complicated interplay between the host, the pathogen, and the environment (Snieszko, 1974).

In aquatic systems, disease management is tough due to the unique ecosystem, where the pathogen is continually waiting for an opportunity when the host's health status is compromised (Sanil et al., 2012). In many cases, disease outbreaks are closely related to environmental deterioration, leading to stress on cultured animals. Different stress factors in the aquatic environment, such as poor water quality, greater microbial load, poor nutritional status, and high stocking density, might increase the risk of infection by opportunistic pathogens (Mishra et al., 2017). The majority of bacterial, parasitic, and fungal pathogens are not completely parasitic. These diseases are extremely adaptable to changes in their environment. If the conditions for parasitism are unsuitable, a saprophytic relationship will develop. Fungal infections can be more common as a result of environmental stressors. High organic loadings were also identified as a cause of increased infection of *Saprolegnia parasitica* (Shaoqi, 1989).

Viral infections, bacterial infections, fungal infections, water mould infections, and other pathogens can cause fish disease (Axelord, 1989). The most common fish diseases, particularly in freshwater, include columnaris, gill disease, ick (ich), dropsy, tail and fin-rot, fungal infections, white spot disease, pop-eye, cloudy eye, and swim bladder disease. Lice, nematode worm infestation, water quality induced diseases, constipation, anorexia, chilodonella, ergasilus, tuberculosis, glugea, henneguya, hexamita, hole-in-the-head disease (head and lateral line erosion disease, lateral line erosion or lateral line disease), injuries, leeches, lymphocystis, marine velvet, and neon-tetra disease, etc. (Aquaticcommunity.com, 2011). The bacterial infections are considered the major cause of mortality in aquaculture. Among the common fish pathogenic bacteria, *Streptococcus agalactiae, Lactococcus garvieae, Enterococcus faecalis (all Gram-positive), Aeromonas hydrophila and Yersinia ruckeri* (both Gram-negative) cause infectious diseases (Pandey et al., 2012).

Fish are exposed to a variety of pollutants in the environment, including medications and chemicals. Different viruses, germs, and parasites can also infect or harm the fish. Chemical contaminants in aquatic environments are a major source of concern because, although it is well understood that aquatic systems are important conduits for the distribution and deposition of many toxic agents, only a few methods exist that provide the sensitivity, accuracy, and practicality required for chemical toxicity assessment. Despite the increasing numbers of synthetic chemicals introduced into the environment each year, concerns remain regarding our understanding of the linkages between exposure to toxic agents and potential disease. As a result, new ways of assessing the health hazards associated with exposure to chemical pollutants in the aquatic environment are required (Madhuri et al., 2012).

The most widespread diseases in fish are those caused by bacteria. Antibiotics are frequently used to treat diseases caused by bacteria, but there is a growing risk of developing antibiotic-resistant bacteria strains. Different herbs have been used safely in organic agriculture, animal medicine, and human medicine to treat bacterial diseases. These herbs mitigate many of the side effects which are associated with synthetic antimicrobials. Furthermore, phyto-medicines generated from plants are less expensive and more precise than chemotherapy drugs. Plants have been utilized as traditional medicine to treat bacterial, viral, fungal, and other infections since time immemorial. Recently, research has been initiated to evaluate the feasibility of herbal drugs for fish diseases (Madhuri et al., 2012).

Ecology is the study of the relationship between organisms, their environments, and with each other. As a result, ecology can include how an organism interacts with and regulates its surroundings. Parasites and other organisms that infect other organisms need to be researched from a variety of angles. Although a parasite's environment is primarily the host organism, the latter is only a small part of the overall larger habitat of the parasite. Parasites are a significant part of every healthy ecosystem. Parasites, like all other organisms, have an ecological niche in which they can thrive. Their niche encompasses the resources and space provided by the host organism's body, as well as the resources and space provided by the host organism's environment.

As a parasite develops an ecological association with a particular host, there may be host specificity but also an immune reaction by the host. The parasite's adaptation to its environment is indicated by site specificity within the host. Parasites are involved in food webs and are part of at least one trophic feeding level since they are a functioning part of an ecosystem. They are always found at a trophic level above their intended hosts, because they use the resources of their hosts to reproduce. Heterotrophic organisms lack the ability to generate their own energy, therefore parasites rely on pre-existing organic molecules to fuel their growth and survival. Although parasites receive energy in the same way as any other heterotrophic creature does, their digestive tracts are frequently simple, allowing for quick and easy absorption.

Freshwater environments serve multiple roles in disease relationships, ranging from a transmission medium for water-borne diseases to a larval habitat for vectors that transmit infections. Warm, moist environments can enhance the persistence of infective stages and facilitate their movement among hosts in three-dimensional space, helping to reduce the challenges of desiccation and local dispersal facing many terrestrial disease agents. Several assumptions regarding the nature of river ecosystems and disease processes were used to build the conceptual framework given here. First, the biosphere is always changing, and these changes have affected and will continue to have an impact on the river's aquatic ecosystems. Second, pathogens are natural ecosystem components. As a result, viruses and hosts adapt in response to one another and to the environment.

As a result, pathogens can exist even when there is no disease. Third, disease prevalence and severity vary across time and space, making it difficult to establish normative conditions, and are influenced by interactions between hosts, pathogens, and the environment, all of which are influenced by a combination of natural and anthropogenic variables. It is our contention that fish health and disease in wild fish populations can be better understood if evaluated in an ecosystem framework rather than in pathogen-centric or host-centric frameworks, which by their nature focus on individual fish. This framework's basic concept is that healthy ecosystems are more likely to be resilient to disease episodes than unhealthy ecosystems (Folke et al., 2004).

Definitions of ecosystem health and ecosystem dysfunction are currently under debate by ecologists (Rapport et al., 1998). The relevance of ecosystem stability and function is consistent with epidemiological principles, which show that the status of the ecosystem influences the frequency and severity of disease events (Hedrick, 1998). For example, temperature, host-immune response, pathogen density, and host population density, for example, are all factors that influence disease transmission. These variables, in turn, are influenced by a large number of ecosystem components, such as climate change, chemical contaminants (which influence host susceptibility and infectivity of pathogens), fishery management actions (harvest and stocking alter host population density), predators, and exotic species (which have the potential to alter host population density and transmission pathways, and may carry new pathogens that are frequently more pathogenic than native hosts).

A healthy ecosystem should have a narrower natural range of temporal and spatial variability for the variables that influence disease transmission. Similarly, in dysfunctional ecosystems, variables that drive disease transmission may show a greater range of variability, thereby increasing the risk that the threshold required for epizootics may be exceeded. In river fishes, disease prevalence and severity are determined by interactions between pathogens, hosts, and the environment, with the latter being the least understood (Hedrick, 1998).

Most pathogens and other disease agents are natural components of ecosystems that can only cause disease under specific environmental conditions. Growing evidence suggests that parasites can have a significant impact on ecosystem structure and function, highlighting the need to integrate disease ecology and ecosystem science. To strengthen links between these traditionally disparate fields, we identified mechanisms through which parasites can affect ecosystems and used empirical literature searches to explore how commonly such mechanisms have been documented, the ecosystem properties affected, and the types of ecosystems in which they occur.

Our review shows that ecosystem-disease research has remained uncommon, accounting for less than 2% of disease ecology papers. According to disease ecologists, have increasingly recognized the potential for parasites to control community structure and shape the outcome of species interactions. Because parasites are unlikely to be equally important in all ecosystems, a goal of our review is to consider when parasites should be incorporated into ecosystem studies, and alternatively, when they can be safely ignored. Finally, we look into future research topics that will help to deepen the linkages between ecosystem science and disease ecology.

In comparison to the marine and terrestrial environments, the importance of disease emergence in freshwater ecosystems has received comparatively less attention (Harvell et al., 1999; Harvell et al., 2002; Lafferty, Porter & Ford, 2004; Ostfeld et al., 2008). Few reviews have widely studied disease patterns in fresh waters outside of human diseases with water-borne (e.g., cholera) or vectorborne (e.g., malaria) transmission (Cotruvo et al., 2004; McNinch, Rose & Dreelin, 2009). Few reviews have broadly explored disease patterns in fresh waters. There have been no studies, especially on wildlife diseases connected with fresh water, that we are aware of. Infectious illness is often overlooked or completely ignored in assessments of developing hazards to freshwater biota (e.g., Dudgeon et al., 2006; Abell et al., 2009).

This raises an important question: are patterns of disease emergence in freshwater habitats less pronounced than in marine or terrestrial ecosystems, for example, owing to differences in ecology, evolution, or anthropogenic influences, or does this trend result instead from a lack of information or synthesis (McCallum et al., 2004; Winfield, 2009). Taxonomic specialization and separation among researchers working on water-related diseases of wildlife (e.g., fishes, crayfishes, amphibians) and humans, for example, could obscure broad-scale patterns in freshwater epidemiology.

Epidemiology is the "study of all ecological aspects of a disease to explain its transmission, distribution, prevalence, and incidence in a population" (Roberts & Janovy, 2005). A parasite's prevalence is influenced by a variety of factors, including host specialization, the ecological environment, and the parasite's capacity to reproduce and disseminate successfully (Roberts & Janovy, 2005). Parasites are a medical problem in many third-world countries. As a result, parasite infection and control approaches are examined regularly and thoroughly. Epidemiological models can be used to examine how different ecological factors affect the population dynamics of pathogens and thus contribute to disease outbreaks (Anderson & May 1991). When considering fish farms as epidemiological units, changes that increase the lifespan of an infection and daily infectiousness can enhance the spread of parasites.

We generally reviewed disease ecology and the complexities inherent to host–pathogen-environment interactions, particularly in the face of rapid and pronounced environmental changes, and the diverse roles of freshwater environments in host–parasite interactions, common types of water-related diseases, their modes of transmission, and the similarities and differences among diseases of freshwater, marine and terrestrial ecosystems.

Researchers often use the ISI Web of Science to analyze the original literature (1970–2009) in fish-related articles of disease in order to quantify the patterns of disease in fresh waters, including temporal trends, major pathogen groups, and impacted host taxa. Finally, threats and challenges facing freshwater ecosystems and how they are likely to influence future patterns and ecosystem services are being reviewed.

Many studies and research have been done in the last few years or so, to understand the molecular biology of fish pathogens, their hosts, and fish diseases caused by pathogens etc. Many studies have been primarily focused on fish diseases and improved diagnostic methods, and on parasite, bacterial, viral, and fungal disease epidemiology (Atinok and Kurt, 2003). Diagnosis of fish has a very important role in solving the problem, as, in some cases, a healthy-looking fish without any clinical symptoms can even carry a disease pathogen that creates a serious risk for the spread of infectious diseases in the fish population. Therefore, new research is very essential for the betterment of fish health due to the exposure of chemical contaminants present in the aquatic environment (Madhuri, et.al.,2012).

Flavobacterium columnare is a bacterial pathogen of freshwater fish that causes skin lesions, fin erosion, and gill necrosis known as columnaris disease. During the last two decades, it has become the most serious threat to salmon (*Salmo salar*) and trout (*Salmo trutta*) smolt and rainbow trout (*Oncorhynchus mykiss*) production in Fennoscandia (Anon. 2009). In the US, columnaris disease causes annual losses of millions of dollars for the channel catfish (*Ictalurus punctatus*) industry (Wagner et al. 2002; Olivares-Fuster et al. 2007). The reasons why this freshwater bacterium has become such a problem for industry are unclear.

The probability of transmission per contact might increase in homogeneous subsets of fish (Ebert 1998), and also in fish stressed by crowding or other environmental factors (Sniezko 1974). The exchange of contaminated material among rearing units can significantly increase the number of hosts available. Recently, we discovered that *F. columnare* may survive for months in sterilized lake water and can colonize fish carcasses (Kunttu et al. 2009). These abilities increase the pathogen's potential to persist in fish tanks when suitable living hosts, for instance, at the end of a rearing cycle or during antibiotic treatments, are temporarily removed.

The use of antibiotics is strictly controlled and regulated due to medication resistance and residue-related problems (Harikrishnan et al., 2011). Production vaccines have played a vital role in the management of infectious diseases in aquaculture for decades in response to the reduced use of antibiotics in fish. Vaccines are widely accepted because of the fact that there is no risk of drug resistance development in vaccinated animals and protection of minority unvaccinated animals because of herd immunity (Gudding et al., 2014). A single approach to aquaculture health prevention and control is ineffective. Rather, a combination of different strategies is effective. It is mandatory to establish a national or regional information exchange between farmers and responsible parties. Aside from implementing all of these techniques, disease surveillance and having sensitive and specific diagnostic tests are essential for ensuring healthy fish.

This review has the aim of summarizing some of the best approaches to prevention and control of infectious diseases of fish in an aquaculture environment.

India is one of the best producers in the world of freshwater fish and is in the ninth position in the ranking of the world's largest freshwater biodiversity among all countries. Trading of fish is not a new thing for India, as every year about 50-60 crore rupees are fetched by the trade. However, the success of breeding of the species in freshwater fish culture directly depends on the health status of the species (Lipton, 2006). About 940 species of freshwater fish are known from lakes, rivers, and estuaries, which is 38.0% of the Ichthyofauna in India. Some of the Indian major carp, viz. Catla, hilsa, mahaseer, mrigal, and rohu are the most preferred species in north India, and snow trout is the most preferred species in north India. Among 940 species, 500 species are mostly found in the Western Ghats and Northern Ghats, and many of these species are reported from forested hills and are unique to certain stretches of various rivers.

Snow trout (*Schizothorax richardsonii*) is a coldwater cyprinid native to the Indian subcontinental Himalayan riverine ecosystems, including adjoining parts of Pakistan, Nepal, and Bhutan (Jhingran, 1991). It is locally known as'

Asala', and it has local importance for its subsistence food fishery. The potential contributing factors responsible for diminishing stocks include destructive and indiscriminate fishing, destruction of general and breeding habitat, low fecundity and slow growth, etc. For these reasons, this species comes under the vulnerable category (Vishwanath, 2010).

Urbanization, deforestation, habitat loss, pollution, over-harvesting, and the culture of exotics are all present threats to indigenous Indian aquatic life, causing many abnormalities and dysfunctions in fish. Pathogens are also a major threat to fishes as they cause many diseases in fish, mainly bacterial, viral, fungal, and parasitic infections. At present time, the population of *Tor* is declining at a fast rate. This declining population of fish raises a lot of questions for biologists, such as whether pollution and many other types of infectious diseases affect its growth performance.

The disease is something which directly affects the fish internally and damages it as a whole and affects the fish mortality rate. The fish mortality rate increases fast in young fishes than in adults. Now, at this point, it becomes a matter of great concern to know further about fish diseases and find ways to cure them properly. In various studies, it is also said that fish get stressed by some environmental imbalances, like natural droughts or pollution, and predators. But in today's world, there are also some other artificial things, like various chemicals, which harm fish a lot. When the waste materials of industries, including chemicals, and household sewage, are added to the rivers, they not only cause diseases in fish, but also reduce the level of oxygen in the water. The reduction of oxygen in the water causes suffocation in many fishes, again causing diseases. Some diseases also cause severe damage to fish farmers' livelihoods.

A great deal of research has been conducted on fish disease over the past century (Mitchell, 2001), but a limited understanding still exists about the risks of disease to natural fish populations (Moffitt et al., 1998). Although disease outbreaks have apparently resulted in significant mortality of wild fish in the Great Lakes (Van Oosten, 1944; Nepszy et al., 1978; Holey et al., 1998; Elsayed et al., 2006; Getchell et al., 2006), the effects on Great Lakes fish populations are difficult to measure and predict. Understanding disease ecology is critical for the long-term viability of wildlife populations, particularly various native fish populations in rivers.

This review was primarily conducted to describe a conceptual framework for fish health that will aid in the development of a fish-friendly ecosystem in Uttarakhand's rivers. Here, we will broadly discuss the relationship between disease ecology and key concepts in ecosystem research.

Integration of parasites and diseases into ecosystem function models is a final strategy that will be valuable in future research. The conceptual framework suggests that disease processes must be considered in an ecosystem context to predict the impact of disease on fish populations, and that the maintenance of ecosystem function may be one way to minimize disease events in natural systems.

REVIEW OF LITERATURE

Diseases of fishes have a long history in terms of literature. Gopalakrishnan and Gupta (1960) found an eye disease which causes mortality of the Catla catla in their research work. Gopalakrishnan (1961) observations on infectious dropsy of Indian major carps as a major disease. Concept of controlling pest and diseases of cultured fishes, given by Gopalakrishnan, (1963). Kumaraiah, et. at. (1971) found a new record of a bacterium causing eye disease and mortality in fishes. Fijan, (1972) first noticed infectious dropsy Diseases in carp fishes Use of terramycin for disease treatment in carp and catfish culture in India by Pal and Tripathi (1970).

Spring viremia of carp (SVC) was very effective, Fijan, N. (1973), while the fungal pathogen of fish was noticed by Ross and Yasutake (1973) in their early days of research. Sniezko, (1974) worked on various environmental stress in relation to diseases of fishes. Bachmann and Ahne, (1974) drew a significant benchmark for biological properties and identification of the agent causing swim bladder inflammation in carp.

Fijan, N. (1975) wrote a note on advances in knowledge of viral diseases of fish. Pal and Ghose (1975) found a method of controlling tail and fin rot disease in Indian major carps during their research. Wolke (1975) noticed that bacterial and fungal diseases can affect fish at the same time. Edwards, and Overstreet, (1976). In their special investigation, they found the tumors of some estuarine fish species. Fungi as a causative agent of disease in fishes was noticed by Ainsworth (1976), and he discusses it in a note entitled "An introduction to the history of mycology".

Ajello et. al. (1977) found a pathogen in rainbow trout and pointed out that the fish was infected by Scolecobasidium humicola. Ahne, (1977) in a significant research notice about a viral disease in fishes. Tesarcik, et. al. (1977) did an electron microscopy study on the form of infectious dropsy of carp. Bucke and Finlay, (1979) research involved identification of spring viraemia in carps. Huizinga et. al. (1979) observed the histopathology of red-sore disease in fishes while working naturally and experimentally. Rhabdovirus infection was noticed in carps during research by Bekesi and Szabo (1979).

Alderman, (1982), and Ellis et. al. (1983) find and focus on fungal disease of aquatic animals and systemic fungal disease respectively. Spring viremia of carp is the most effective disease observed by Bootsma and Ebregt (1983). Spring viremia of carp virus (SVCV) was also noticed by Faisal and Ahne, (1984). Pathogens and the environment in European polyculture focused by Fijan, (1984). Cusack and Cone (1986) described the parasites as vectors of viral and bacterial diseases in fish. Field and Laboratory Investigations into Ulcerative Fish Diseases noticed by Roberts, et al. (1986). Dropsy is one of the most dominant diseases of Catla catla that affects cultural biology by Kumar, et. at. (1986).

Kumar, et. at. (1986) research findings explore the preliminary observations of gill hyperplasia in common carp and Kumar, et. at. (1987 a) talks about ulcerative disease in Catla catla. Wolf K. (1988), studied fish viruses and fish viral diseases. Hawkins, et. al. (1988) proposed small fish models for identifying carcinogens in the aqueous environment. Egusa S. (1991) and Anonymous (1991) talk about fungal diseases and the health of aquaculture animals respectively. Hill B. (1992) noticed the great impact of viral diseases on salmonid fish in Europe that caused huge economic damage.

Kirpichnikov, et al. (1993) research on common carp and working towards resistance to dropsy in common carp was shown. Water fungus and mold infectious to freshwater fishes were observed during research by Noga (1993). Environmental factors affecting the outbreaks of fish disease in various cases were specially focused by Bly, et. al. (1993). Avtalion, and Shlapobersky, (1994) found a viral disease of tilapia larvae, whereas Crow, et. al. (1995) noticed a Fusarium solani fungal infection of the lateral line canal of the fish. The relationship between fish pathogen and host was clearly established by Yuasa and Hati (1995).

Meng et. at. (1996) talks about disease and provides a solution for chemical prevention and treatment of seasonal diseases. Kitancharoen et. at. (1997) found some aquatic fungi defect on salmonids. Lilley, and Inglis (1997) show comparative effects of various antibiotics, fungicides, and disinfectants on fish, whereas Dixon, (1997) talks about viral diseases of carp and catfish. Hedrick, (1998) stablished the relationships between the host, pathogen, and the environment, and Gonzalez, et. al. (1997) showed the detection of the infectious hematopoietic necrosis virus directly from infected fish tissues. Moffitt, et. at. (1998) isolated the pathogens and found diseases of fish in aquatic ecosystems during research.

Khoo et al., (1998) work on Branchiomyces infection in catfish and gave impactful findings in the field of fish disease. Olesen N.J. (1998) research on the sanitation of viral haemorrhagic septicaemia (VHS), whereas the chronic infection in Indian major carp, Catla catla, was observed by Shome and Shome (1999). Aoki (1999) did significant work on fish diseases and disorders.

Moving towards recent years, various research is still continuing in the field of fish disease. Mohan and Bhatta, (2002) establish a relationship between the social and economic impacts of aquatic animal health. research in this field was done by Mukherjee, (2002) and published in a book entitled 'Fish diseases in India'. Spring viremia of carp is a noticeable disease in fishes, as shown by Ahne, et. al. (2002). Ariel & Olesen, (2002) research on aquaculture and related diseases. Wagner, et. al. (2002) studied the epidemiology of bacterial disease in catfish. Harvell et al. (2002) opened a new area of research in the field of fish disease. That was, Climate warming and disease risks for terrestrial and marine biota.

Altinok & Kurt, (2003) studied the molecular diagnosis of fish diseases, whereas Cotruvo, et al. (2004) worked on the causes and control of fish diseases. Jeremic, et. at. (2004) found out the dissemination of spring viraemia of carp (SVC). Rhabdo viruses cause significant damage to fishes. Hoffmann, et. al. (2005). Bondad-Reantaso, et al. (2005) point out the need for proper health management in aquaculture that can be affected by fish disease, whereas the epidemiological approach to fish health management by Subasinghe, (2005). Parveen, et. al. (2005) observed seasonal variation in diseases in indigenous fishes.

Lipton, (2006), noticed the diseases of ornamental fishes and their control. Dudgeon et al. (2006) observe freshwater biodiversity status and conservation in relation to fish disease. OIE (2006) proposed a manual of tests for aquatic animal disease diagnostic methods. Olivares-Fuster, et. al. (2007) in a notable work shows a host-specific association between pathogens and fish species. Austin (2007) found bacteria as a fish pathogen, and main causative agent of disease Dixon, (2008) give the idea about virus diseases of cyprinids, whereas American Veterinary Medical Association (2008) took an initiative about 'one health initiative task force Fish Immunology' in relation to diseases of fishes.

Kunttu, et. at. (2009) fish pathogens as a transmission strategy for diseases of fishes. Abell et. al. (2009) talks about the conservation of aquatic ecosystems. A significant work by Bassey, (2011) and published a book about parasitology and fish disease. Peeler and Taylor, (2011) research on epidemiology in aquatic animal health. Disease in relation to the environment was stabilised by Dixon, et al. (2012), and found out the effect of temperature and pH on the inactivation of fish viral and bacterial pathogens. Use of medicine to treat fish disease by Romero et. at. (2012) and find out about antibiotics in aquaculture and their alternatives.

Madhuri et. at. (2012). Antimicrobial activity of some medicinal plants against fish pathogens. Recently, the spring viremia of carp a virus disease was noticed by Phelps, et al. (2012). Pandey et. al. (2012) show the effect of medicinal plants on fish disease treatment. Sahoo, et al. (2013), and Bagum, et al.

(2013) stabilised the economic basis of fish disease in freshwater aquaculture. 'Vaccination as a Preventive Measure' in Fish disease, a research-oriented statement given by Gudding, (2014). Misk, et al. (2016) noticed the pathogenesis of spring viremia in carp, and in the same year (Sandeep, 2016), observed parasitic and bacterial diseases in fresh water fish. (2017) fish disease management in freshwater aquaculture in India and Sen, and Mandal, (2018) research on fresh-water fish diseases in West Bengal, India.

Bataillon and Terre, (1897) were the first researchers who recorded fish diseases when they reported their occurrence in carp species (*Cyprinus carpio*) in water which was contaminated by the excreta of a tuberculous person. Some workers observed the disease in the same fish (*Gadus callaria*) and described the pathology of the infection. Alexender obtained bacteria from the dark-coloured skin area to find out some results, but he was unsuccessful in culturing it. Some researchers also conducted experiments to determine the origin of the bacteria and they also claimed that fish had adopted bacteria tubercle bacillus from humans, but the researchers were unsuccessful (Bataillon and Terre, 1902).

Hines, et.al. (1947) gave a report on the protozoan disease ichthyophthiriasis in goldfish indicating that different species of fish show different ability to resist the disease. Also, Clayton and Price, (1992) demonstrated that different strains of platy, an aquarium fish, show different types of susceptibility to ICH. Anderson (1974) found out that young fish are more susceptible to the pathogen because of their immature immune systems. In 1963, Gopalakrishnan stated that to cure the bacterial disease fin and tail rot, it was necessary to dip infected fish in a 1:2000 solution of copper sulphate solution. This research on fish has found great results, which help us to know even more about many things.

Gopalakrishnan (1963) and Hora and Pillay (1962) had reported fin-rot bacterial disease in both young and adult fishes. They also said that the disease is also capable of causing serious damage and financial loss to fish farmers. However, both of them failed to find any particular pathogen for this disease. Further studies into bacterial disease and many scientists have reported that *A. hydrophila* and pseudomonas fluorescens cause this bacterial infection. Many workers, scientists, and researchers have also suggested some controlling measures for this disease, as also suggested by Gopalakrishnan in his study, like bath treatment of infected fish with 1:2000 copper sulphate solution for 2-4 minutes.

In a study done by Gopalkrishnan (1961) and Kumaraiah (1971), another bacterial disease was reported which was an infection of *A.liquifaciens* which infects mainly the eyes of cats. This infection may also lead to the death of fish because of complete necrosis. Jhingran (1991) in his study also observed this similar type of infection many years after that in *Channa Marulius*. Some workers had to find out that a Chloromycetin bath is a very effective way to control this disease.

Kumar et. al., (1986), reported a condition of myxobacterial organisms known as gill hyperplasia syndrome, which mostly infects the common carp (*Cyprinus carpio*). For years, some workers conducted antibiotic therapy to learn more about the infectious nature of this disease, but they could not find a significant result. Kumar, et. al., (1986), also described a similar disease called gill hyperplasia syndrome, which causes lesions over the entire body surface of infected fish. The causative organism for this disease has been identified as *Flexibacter columnaris*. To cure this disease, a short bath of KMnO4 and application of potassium permanganate have been found to be really effective.

Dropsy is another bacterial disease in India which mostly affects freshwater fish species like rohu, mrigal, and catla in the late winter season. Several workers have reported that in this disease, the body cavity of fish gets filled with fluid and the body scales protrude, which can also lead to anemic condition.

Pal and Tripathi (1970) have reported that the occurrence of this disease is also present in fish culture ponds. They also treated the affected fish. Kumar, et. al., (1986) reported a type of infection which is caused by a mixed infection of myxosporidian parasites and *A.hydrophila* in *Catla catla.*

Many workers reported ulcerative disease in *catla* where they found bilateral ulcerations of the head and the opercula. In many cases, the penetration of opercular bones and the cranium has been reported due to ulcerations. Gopalakrishnan (1963) and one other researcher, Karunasagar et. al., (1986), have reported such outbreaks. Kumar et. al., (1987) also reported this condition in a composite fish culture pond in his study. Mukherjee et. al., (1991) found out the role of *A.hydrophila* in the ulcerative disease of fish and also identified the biochemical differences among the different strains. A study of biochemical properties and antibiograms was also conducted by Nayak and Mukherjee (1994) based on antibiotic sensitivity tests.

Kumar, et. al., (1989), isolated several bacterial pathogens, viz. *Aeromonas punctata, A.hydrophila, Pseudomonas* sp., *Streptococcus* sp., and *Flavobacterium* sp., from infected specimens. Dey (1989), reported in one of his histological studies, that there is a complete loss of epidermis in the area of ulceration. In the traditional period, diagnosis of fish disease was carried out by histological examination or by the cultivation of agar and serological and phenotypic properties of the pathogen (Bernardet et al., 1990; Pazos et al. (1996). Histological experiments were unsuccessful in identifying some of the bacteria because of their similar structures.

Furthermore, some attempts have been made to the diagnosis of fish diseases like DNA homology, biochemical tests, protease variability, etc., (Pyle and Shotts, (1980); Bertolini and Rohovec (1992); Chen et al., (1995)), but there are some disadvantages to these techniques. Many different methods and techniques have also been tried to control diseases. Several antibiotics, chemicals, sulfonamides, and herbal preparations have been reported as curative and preventive measures. Fish farmers in the country have accepted the use of lime until the scientists of CIFA formulate medicine for disease. Records have revealed that there has been no occurrence of any disease for atleast 10-11 months where medicine is applied. These techniques have been used by many workers, like Prichard, (1997); McKeand, (1998); Altinok and Kurt, (2003), Gonzalez, et. al., (1997) for the diagnosis of parasitic, bacterial, fungal, and viral infections in fish.

BACTERIAL DISEASE

[3.1] INTRODUCTION OF BACTERIAL DISEASES

Bacterial fish diseases are very widespread and are one of the most difficult health concerns to deal with. These bacteria are usually saprophytic in nature and can only be pathogenic if the fishes have physiological imbalances, nutritional deficiencies, or if there are other stressors, i.e., poor water quality, overstocking, which allow opportunistic bacterial infections to proceed (Sandeep et al., 2016). In the aquaculture industry, bacterial pathogens, particularly *Aeromonas* spp., cause severe losses and pose a possible threat to human health. *A. hydrophila* is a gram-negative aerobic, opportunistic, oxidase-positive motile bacterium that inhabits aquatic environments. It is often seen with poultry, fish, milk, and red meat (Roberts, 1993, Aoki, 1997). It mainly causes disease and mortality in freshwater fishes, sometimes in marine fishes (Aoki, 1999).

Humans are also infected by the bacteria, which produces symptoms ranging from gastroenteritis to septicaemia (Sha et al., 2002). As a result, the organism is considered a threat to human health and fish. The presence of motile aeromonads in the freshwater ecosystem suggests that they have a role in epizootics and secondary infections associated with EUS outbreaks (Bhowmik et al., 2009). This bacterium is also responsible for the condition known as 'Red Sore Syndrome' (Huizinga et al., 1979). In general, *A. hydrophila* does not cause difficulties in fish populations unless the fish are stressed by the environment or are infected with other infections (Fang et al., 2000).

Mortalities from hydrophila infection were recorded in the South and South-East Asia (Roberts, 2005), while (Musa et al., 2008) stated that bacterial isolates from sick freshwater ornamental fish from aquarium shops in Terengganu, Malaysia were found to Malaysia consists of 60 percent of *A. hydrophila* and cause diverse pathologic conditions such as dermal ulceration, rotting of the tails, fin haemorrhage, septiceamia, red sores, exophthalmia, erythrodermatitis and scale protrusion, especially in common carp, *Cyprinus carpio* (Cipriano et al., 2001; Austin, 2007). Chronic infections could lead to ulceration, inflammation and dermal lesions with focal haemorrhages (Cipriano et al., 2001) and during acute septicaemia, the liver and kidney are the common target organs (Huizinga et al., 1979). A highly virulent strain of *A. hydrophila* was reported from the Indian major carp, *catla catla* from Andaman (Shome, 1999). The present paper represents the results of pathogenecity and histopathological alterations of Indian Major Carps *L. rohita*, experimentally infected with *A. hydrophila*.

Bacterial diseases have been encountered often in eggs, fry, and fingerlings of fish, resulting in high mortality. These bacteria are opportunistic pathogens that infect the tissues of a fish host that has been rendered vulnerable to infection by stress conditions (Parveen et. al. 2005). The occurrence of bacterial diseases was not considered to be a serious problem in our country, as economic losses in fish culture were not known. The incidences of Ulcerative disease (EUS) in various Southeast Asian countries, as well as in India, have focused tremendous attention on the threat the disease epidemics hold for farmers. Economic losses of the order of US $ 10 million in Thailand and over $3 million in Bangladesh were lessons enough to realize their importance (Mukherjee, 2002). Some of the important bacterial diseases, like motile aeromonads septicaemia caused by *Aeromonas hydrophila*, edwardsiellosis caused by *Edwardsiella tarda*, Pseudomonas septicaemia by *Pseudomonas fluorescens* and *Pseudomonas putrefaciens*, flexibacteriosis by *Flexibacter columnar*, Vibriosis by *Vibrio alginolyticus* and *V. parahaemolyticus* bacterial gill disease, streptococcal septicaemia, mycobacteriosis, and enteric septicaemia, are often reported in carp culture in India (Mukherjee, 2002; Mohanty and Sahoo, 2007).

According to Sandeep et al., 2016 and Das et al., 2011, there are four types of bacterial infections. i) Fin rot-usually resulting from environmental stress,

ii) Bacterial body ulcers-open, shallow to deep, lesions on the fish's body, iii) Bacterial gill disease-in which the gills are the primary target iv) Systemic bacterial disease, in which bacteria invade and cause damage to internal organs. Another bacterial disease commonly reported in fish culture is bacterial skin disease or red disease. It is a systematic bacterial infection. On the fish's body, there are red spots, a depression with bulging eyes, and an abdomen. A diverse range of microorganisms are involved, the majority of which are Gram-negative rods. Many pathogens are present only in skin lesions, especially *Flexibacteria, Aeromonads*, Vibrios etc. There may be necrotic lesions on the fins (fin rot).

The disease may become a systematic, more severe form, causing mortality. Motile *Aeromonas Septicaemia* is another important bacterial disease in carp culture that is frequently mistaken for red sickness (MAS). This is the most frequent bacterial illness in freshwater fish culture, causing severe production losses. Several Aeromonas species, including *A. hydrophila, A. sobria, A. caviae, A. schuberti, and A.veronii*, have been linked to this condition (Mohanty and Sahoo, 2007). The clinical signs of motile *Aeromonas septicaemia* include high morbidity, often with superficial to deep skin lesions, and sometimes sudden death with or without any clinical symptoms. Skin lesions are often noticed at the base of the fins, with variously sized areas of haemorrhage and necrosis. The disease is sometimes referred to as "red-disease" since it causes red spots on the body, skin ulcers, a swollen abdomen, and enlarged eyes and muscles. These lesions may progress to reddish to grey ulcers with underlying tissue necrosis. If quick intervention is not taken, the fatality rate can easily exceed 100%.

Fish are susceptible to a variety of bacterial diseases, especially if they are kept in high-density environments. Disease outbreaks increase mortality and reduce productivity, resulting in significant financial losses for fish farmers (Madhuri and Mandloi, 2012). Streptococcosis, lactococcosis, haemorrhagic septicemia (HS), and ulcers in the fins are all caused by bacteria belonging to the *S.agalactiae, L. garvieae*, and *E. faecalis* families (Buller, 2004). When compared to other aquatic bacteria, *Flavobacterium columnare* is harmful only to freshwater fish species and has low environmental fitness. Despite this, this agent is extremely dangerous to young fish (fry and fingerlings), producing skin lesions and significant mortality, which is usually linked to poor environmental conditions (Grabowshi et al., 2004).

Enteric red mouth disease, mostly restricted to salmonids, is caused by *Y. ruckeri*, the most prevalent symptom being reddened mouth and throat (Austin, 2007). *A. hydrophila* is responsible for cases of skin infections, septicemia, and gastroenteritis in fish and humans (Yu BH, 2007). *A. hydrophila* is known to be the most prevalent bacterial pathogen in freshwater fish, which has various different aetiological disorders, including tail/fin rot, motile *Aeromonas septicemia* (MAS) or HS, and epizootic ulcerative syndrome (EUS) as a primary pathogen. EUS is a globally distributed disease and is an epidemic, affecting a variety of wild and cultured fish species, especially in Southeast Asia, including Pakistan and India (Pandey, 2012; Abdul et al., 2011).

The common bacterial diseases prevalent among fishes in India are not well studied. In Uttarakhand, knowledge about bacterial fish diseases is still unknown, which mostly affects the livelihoods of fish farmers. Literature regarding fish diseases is also not found to a great extent, which necessitates the study of diseases in fishes to provide knowledge to all upcoming researchers and for fish farmers, for whom fish are the only source of their livelihood.

[3.2] TYPES OF BACTERIAL DISEASES

[3.2.1] FIN AND TAIL ROT FIN DISEASE

Fin rot and tail rot diseases are very common in freshwater fishes, mostly in sewage-fed fisheries. In the infected fish with this disease, the tail and fin get discoloured. This is mainly caused by mixed infections with *Aeromonas hydrophila* and *Pseudomonas fluzrescens.* Improvements in water quality and a reduction in stocking density are essential for long-term management of the disease. Both adults and young fish are affected. The early stage infection is a white line on the edge of the fine, spreading and imparting a frayed appearance to the appendage that eventually disintegrates and spills out. This disease is contagious and may cause considerable damage (Jhingran, 1991).

[3.2.2] ULCER DISEASE (COLUMNARIS DISEASE)

This disease is also known as ulcer disease, which is caused by *Chondroccus columnaris*, in freshwater fish. *Flavobacterium columnare* is a bacterial pathogen of freshwater fish causing skin lesions, fin erosion, and gill necrosis known as columnaris disease. This disease is caused by *Flexibactor columnaris* and shows raised white plaques, often with a reddish peripheral zone, leading to haemorrhagic ulcers (Jhingran, 1991). It has become the most serious threat to salmon (*Salmo salar*), trout (*Salmo trutta*), and rainbow trout (*Oncorhynchus mykiss*) smolt and rainbow trout (*Oncorhynchus mykiss*) production in Fennoscandia over the last two decades (Anon. 2009). The channel catfish (*Ictalurus punctatus*) industry in the United States loses millions of dollars each year due to columnaris disease (Wagner et al. 2002; Olivares-

Fuster et al. 2007). It's not obvious why this bacterial infection has become such a concern for industry.

We consider that the arguments above make a strong case that the evolution of *F. columnare* towards higher virulence is one reason why columnaris disease has become such a problem for the industry. Our arguments, however, are correlational or original. It would, of course, be more decisive to prove that genetic mutation took place and is accountable for the increasing prevalence and severity of diseases. Unfortunately, in the early years of the survey, attempts at the *F. columnare* culture were not effective. This failure could be due to virulence evolution: it's still difficult to isolate non-virulent strains from natural populations or even experimentally infected fish, which prohibits us from conducting cross-infection investigations with *F. columnare* strains from farmed and wild fish. In the absence of such direct evidence, other explanations for the increase in F. columnare incidence are possible.

Domestication could, for example, lead to a greater vulnerability to diseases in farmed fish. There has been no growth in the incidence of four other bacterial diseases, such as *aeromonas salmonicida*, typic *A. salmonicida, Yersinia ruckeri,* and *Serratias sp*. These bacteria, as *F. columnare* is the case, are treated at the beginning of the disease with disease-specific medications, but they don't have the biological properties, as we know. In particular, they do not transmit via dead fish, and there is no evidence for these diseases that virulence and infectivity are linked.

[3.2.3] DROPSY

Dropsy is not an actual disease, but a physical manifestation of kidney failure in fish, where the fish's body balloons outward from excess water and its scales stick out like a pine cone. But dropsy disease can be possible through bacterial infection. A freshwater fish exists in a hypotonic environment. It is a disease caused by bacterial infection which directly affects the kidneys, resulting in renal failure and fluid accumulation. The name of the bacteria which causes this disease is *Pseudomonas punctata.* Dropsy is another bacterial disease in India which mostly affects freshwater fish species like rohu, mrigal, and catla in the late winter season. Several workers have reported that in this disease, the body cavity of fish gets filled with fluid and the body scales protrude, which can also lead to anemic condition.

Dropsy is a condition in fish caused by the buildup of fluid inside the body cavity or tissues. As a symptom rather than a disease in its own right, it can indicate a number of underlying diseases, including bacterial infections, parasitic infections, or liver dysfunction. Pal and Tripathi (1970) have reported that the occurrence of this disease is also present in fish culture ponds. They also treated the affected fish.

Kumar, et. al., (1986) reported a type of infection which is caused by a mixed infection of *myxosporidian* parasites and *A.hydrophila* in *Catla catla.*

That is, freshwater is made up of a higher concentration of water and a lower concentration of solutes, like salt. This causes water to travel freely in the skin of the fish and other tissues, as well as in the body. The water must also leave its body, else the fish will absorb lethal water. The kidneys remove excess water, pushing it through the gills and urine tract out of the body and into the environment. However, the excess water can build up internally if your kidney does not function appropriately and so leads to the bloated appearance known as dropsy. A sign of excess water retention may be from a slight rounding of the belly to a very swollen belly. In such a disease, fluid accumulation inside the body cavity, scale protrusion, exophthalmic condition, and inflammation of the intestine (Gopalakrishnan, 1961) and haemorrhagic ulcers occur on the skin and fins (Jhingran, 1991).

[3.2.4] EYE DISEASE

This disease is caused by a bacterium, *Aeromonas liquifaciens*. The freshwater fish species "*Catla catla*" is the most commonly affected fish species by this epidemic eye disease. This epidermal eye condition affecting the Indian carp *Catla catla* was first identified by Gopalakrishnan in 1960. As the name explains, the infected sites for this disease are the eyes.

This is a widespread eye disease that affects both medium and large catla fish. This disease is caused by a bacterium variant, *Aeromonas liquefaciens*. The eyes, optic nerves, and brain of the fish are all infected locations (Gopalakrishnan, 1961; Gopalakrishnan, 1960).

[3.3] DIAGNOSIS OF BACTERIAL DISEASES

Diagnosis is a medical condition in which a disease is identified by its symptoms and signs by using various diagnostic methods. This diagnosis helps the researcher to recognize a disease by its outmost symptoms and signs and also to analyze the physiological and biochemical causes of the disease. Disease diagnosis is a method which is used to analyze the cause and nature of a disease. Proper diagnosis helps in the proper treatment of disease and avoids unnecessary use of different chemotherapeutics.

Eye observation is one of the very first methods of disease diagnosis. We can simply observe different symptoms and signs of infection without any proper equipment or instruments. This foremost method used in disease diagnosis was proper case history information, which helps to know the cause of disease development. Some of the methods used in this literature were to check water quality, feeding percentage, swimming behavior, stocking details, etc. These are the basic procedures for disease diagnosis to know the nature of the disease and how it developed.

Researchers use some equipment for the diagnosis of fish diseases. One of the most needed equipment for this was a high-quality microscope having lenses of 10X, 40X, and 100X objectives. Some other basic equipment which was required included simple surgical instruments like scalpels, fine and coarse scissors, fine and coarse forceps, disposable gloves, and 10% formalin solution. Other materials which were required include clean 30–40 liters of water, plastic buckets, various-sized aquarium bags, and an aquarium container with a small air pump (available from a local aquarium shop). Identification of infected fishes was mostly done by the researchers with the help of (Jhingran, 1991).

[3.4] BACTERIAL DISEASE TREATMENT

For fin and tail rot diseases, a one-minute dip in a 1:3,000 solution of copper sulphate should be given (Gopalakrishnan, 1963). Painting the infection location with a strong copper sulphate solution also aids in the treatment (Pal, 1975). In the case of ulcer disease, the severely infected fish should be removed, and the pond water disinfected with a 0.5 ppm KMnO4 solution. In the case of fish displaying early signs of infection, a one-minute dip in a 1:2,000 copper sulphate solution is necessary for 3 to 4 days. Chloromycetin is added to the pond water at a concentration of 5 to 10 ppm, or the antibiotic oxytetracycline is added to the feed at a concentration of 75 mg/kg of fish per day. In the case of dropsy, a thorough disinfection with a 1 ppm potassium permanganate solution or a 2-minute plunge in a 5-ppm solution of the same chemical might be provided. A chloromycetin (8-10 mg/L) bath should be given for 2 to 3 days during the initial stage of infection in eye disease. Disinfection of the pond with 1 ppm potassium permanganate, improved sanitary conditions, and artificial fish feeding (if the plankton population is insufficient) should all be done (Gopalakrishnan, 1960).

[3.4.1] FIN AND TAIL ROT DISEASE

Researchers generally treated the infected fish with chloromphenicol antibiotics. Adding to the water, generally 20-30mg per liter. If the fish is to be treated, antibiotics can be further added to the food. With flake food, researchers use about 1% of antibiotics and carefully mix them in. If you retain the fish, they must eagerly eat the mixture before the antibiotic dissipates.

[3.4.2] DROPSY TREATMENT

Generally, bacterial infected fishes were treated with the above treatment procedure, which was also earlier used by many other researchers. These treatments have been found to be really effective and also at a low cost. An effective treatment or prevention of this disease is done by removing the infected fish followed by draining, drying and disinfecting the pond with lime. These are preventive measures to control the disease. Penicillin and chloromphenicol antibiotics are also very effective for treating diseases like fin and tail rot and columnaris disease. The treatment and preventive measures for some diseases like Dropsy, Branchiomycosis, and Icthyophonus are done by removing the infected fish followed by draining, drying, and disinfecting with lime.

[3.4.2] COLUMNARIS DISEASE

For prevention of this disease, many researchers have found that treating infected fish with penicillin at 10,000 units per liter is an effective treatment for preventing this sickness. A second dose will be given in two days. Other antibiotics may be effective as well. There were no significant modifications in farming operations during this time, with the exception of the introduction of antibiotics (oxytetracyclin) in 1993, which were used against columnaris outbreaks. Fish were observed for clinical signs of columnaris disease, and symptoms were recorded by most previous workers. Bacteria were isolated from infected tissues (fins, gills, skin and, from 2004 onwards, also from the kidney) on Anacker and Ordal agar (Anacker & Ordal 1955). Tissue scrapings from infected tissue were also taken on microscopic slides. The slides were air-dried, Gram-stained and inspected for the presence of long rod-shaped bacteria using a microscope at 1000-fold magnification by Anacker and Ordal, 1955.

The symptoms of columnaris were categorised according to their intensity in five categories. In decreasing order of severity, the categories included: necrosis, erosion or inflammation of tissue in (i) gills (ii) jaws (iii) saddleback area (iv) tail (v) skin. Previous researchers studied fish infection before possible antibiotic treatment.

[3.4.4] EYE DISEASE

In the early infection of this disease, a Chloromycetin bath was a very effective method of controlling this disease, but in the case of higher infection, the eyes get putrified, which leads to the death of the fish.

[3.5] SUMMARY

The table and figure given below summarises all bacterial diseases, including symptoms and causal microorganisms.

Table 1. Bacterial diseases

Sl No	Disease Condition	Symptoms	Involvement of Pathogens
1	Fin and Tail rot Disease	Erosions, discolorations and disintegration of fins and tails.	*Aeromonas salmonici*

2	Dropsy	Haemorrhagic lesions on skin, fins, tail	*Pseudomonas punctata*
3	Columnaris Disease	Haemorrhagic and ulcerative lesions on fins, head, back, which may look yellow to orange.	*Chondroccus columnaris*
4	Eye disease	Cataract of eyes affect the cornea, eyeball gets putrefied	*Aeromonas liquifaciens*

Figure 1. Bacterial diseases, (A) Fin and Tail rot Disease, (B) Dropsy, (C) Columnaris Disease, (D) Eye disease

FUNGAL DISEASE

[4.1] INTRODUCTION OF FUNGAL DISEASES

Only a few fungal species are known to be harmful to fish, in contrast to bacterial and parasitic infections. These are usually found in water and attack fish under unfavorable conditions, causing skin lesions. The oomycete fungi, Saprolegnia, Achlya, and Aphanomyces, are responsible for the majority of fungal infections observed in carp culture. This disease is induced by this fungus, known as "saprolegniasis" (Mishra et. al, 2017). These oomycete fungi are widely found in aquatic habitats but are rarely thought of as major pathogens.

These are commonly characterised as saprophytic, opportunistic secondary pathogens that quickly colonize bacterium or parasite-infected tissues (Mukherjee, 2002). Fungal growths on skin or fins look like patches of white to whitish-grey cotton-wool like growths. The majority of these are made up of many fungal hyphae that may be seen under a microscope. Saprolegniasis is particularly common in over-wintering ponds with high stocking density, such as those used in cage culture or intensive aquaculture. Although there have been several reports of saprolegniasis mostly in cage culture systems, the incidences in pond culture systems are usually lower, unless there is chronic mismanagement. Besides

Saprolegnia, Branciomyces and Aphanomyces cause disease in pond aquaculture.

Epizootic Ulcerative Syndrome is another prominent fungal-induced disease in fish production that has a high economic impact (EUS). It has spread throughout freshwater farming, resulting in significant losses throughout Southeast Asia, including India. It's a serious and economically significant disease that affects farmed freshwater fish, and it's a notifiable disease. On the body's surface, hemorrhages and ulcers are clinical symptoms of this disease. It is a serious bacterial-fungal infection that causes substantial mortality in freshwater fish. *Catla catla, L. rohita, C. mrigala, C. carpio, Channa sp., Puntus sp.,* and *G. chapra* are among the most commonly affected fish species (Mishra, et al. 2017).

Affected fish grow feeble, malnourished, and float on the water's surface. On the skin, reddish-brown lesions, often with hemorrhages, appear at first, then get deeper and take the appearance of ulcers. In some cases, tissue patches fall off, resulting in secondary infection and a high mortality rate (Mishra et al., 2017). Although a wide variety of organisms have been isolated from the body surfaces and internal organs of the fish, *Aphanomyces invadrans* is believed to be the primary causative organism. Fish may be predisposed to infection by a variety of biotic and abiotic causes (Bagum et al., 2013). They reported the most common disease in Bangladesh that has a significant impact on carp culture. They indicated that ponds receiving water from rice fields and rivers had a high relative risk of fungal disease (Bagum et al., 2013).

Farmers in the region use probiotic formulations, aqua medicines and chemicals, various antimicrobials, sanitizers, anti-parasitic drugs, and even antibiotics in their fish culture systems, as preventive and control measures to protect the crops. Fish farming uses some of the same medications and preparations that are used in animal treatment and agriculture (Mishra et al., 2017). CIFAX, a chemical formulation developed by ICAR-CIFA scientists, has been found to be quite effective in suppressing and controlling fish infections, as well as having other beneficial effects on pond culture (Anon, 2017). Saprolegniasis, branchiomycosis, and idiopathic fungus are the three most frequent fungal disorders.

Aquatic animals, like vertebrates, are susceptible to a wide range of pathogenic pathogens, including fungi. The earliest clinical record of a fungus infecting a vertebrate was actually of a fish (Ainsworth, 1976). There are currently a number of well-written, in-depth reviews, chapters, and even volumes devoted just to the issue of fungal infections of aquatic organisms (Alderman, 1982; Willoughby, 1994). This review should not be viewed as a replacement for these outstanding resources, but it will hopefully serve to highlight and complement a few of them, as well as provide the latest information available on this subject. In comparison to other animals, fish are only affected by a small number of fungus. Fungal infections in fish are most commonly caused by members of the Saprolegniaceae family, which belongs to the class of Oomycetes, or water moulds. (1982, Alderman). The following taxonomy, which is a mix of published schemas, lists these and other fungi important in causing fish diseases (Egusa, 1991; Roberts, 1989).

Many of the fungi that affect fish, especially those in the Saprolegniaceae family, are considered opportunists. They attack fish when they are stressed or become immunocompromised due to adverse environmental conditions, or secondary to bacterial or viral infections, when they have lost their mucus protection because of trauma or excessive handling (Neish, 1980; Bly et al., 1993; Quiniou et al., 1998; Roberts, 1989). There are, however, primary pathogens even in the family Saprolegniaceae that cause disease without predisposing factors (Neish, 1980; Roberts, 1989).

[4.2] TYPES OF FUNGAL DISEASES

[4.2.1] SAPROLEGNIASIS

Saprolegniasis is the most widely accepted collective term for fungal infections of fish and fish eggs caused by members of the genera Saprolegnia, Achyla, and Dictyuchus (Roberts, 1989; Post, 1987); Neish, 1980; Roberts, 1989; Post, 1987). It has long been suspected of being a key component in salmon disease (Neish, 1980). It is also sometimes referred to as fish fungus disease or fungus disease (mainly in ornamental fish) (Post, 1987) or as winter fungus when it is associated with winter kill syndrome in the channel catfish industry. (Bly et al., 1993; Tucker and Robinson, 1990; Meng et al., 1996). *Saprolegnia parasitica* is the cause of this infection. The fertilized eggs in hatching 'hapas' are frequently infected by this fungus. The fungus begins by attacking the dead eggs and then spreads to the remaining viable eggs, spoiling them as well (Jhingran, 1991).

[4.2.2] BRANCHIOMYCOSIS (GILL ROT)

It is caused by the fungi, *Branchiomyces sanguinis* (in carps) and *Branchiomyces demigrans* (in pike and tench). Branchiomycosis is a widespread disease in the United States, although it has only been reported in India on a few occasions. Fish suffering from environmental stress, such as low pH (5.8-6.5), low dissolved oxygen, or a high algal bloom, are found to have both types of fungal. Branchiomyces sp. grows at temperatures ranging from 57° F and 95° F, but grows best between 77° F and 90° F. Fungal spores transported in the water and detritus on pond bottoms are the main causes of infection. *B. sanguinis* and *B. demigrans* infect the gill tissue of infected fish. Fish may appear lethargic and may be seen swallowing air from the water surface (or piping). Gills appear to be striated or marbled, with pale regions indicating infection or dying tissue. A professional diagnostician should inspect the gills under a microscope to confirm the condition. There will be fungal hyphae and spores in the damaged gill tissue. The spores are discharged into the water as the tissue dies and falls off, and they are spread to other fish. This infection is frequently linked to high mortality rates (Klinger, 1996).

Branchiomycos, also known as gill rot, is an acute, localized fungal infection of the gill that affects a wide range of freshwater fish (Neish, 1980; Egusa, 1991). It has been documented in India and in number of other countries (the United States, Japan, Indochina, Israel, and Europe), where it is regarded a major problem in commercial fish production (Neish, 1980; Egusa, 1991, Wolke, 1975). Although two species of Branchiomyces are recognized, namely *B. sanguinis* and *B. demigrans,* this remains in contention, as is their classification. Based on gel precipitation experiments and spore shape, some have proposed they belong to the order Saprolegniales (Alderman, 1982). *B. demigrans* possesses stronger hyphal walls and larger spores, as well as a tendency to grow outside of blood arteries, which distinguishes it from other species (Neish, 1980). Some argue that these morphological differences and growth tendencies may be the function of the host and environment rather than actual species differences.

As fish with subacute to acute infections most often experience respiratory discomfort or lethargy, as it causes respiratory injury (Post, 1987). These epizootics usually develop if water temperatures are higher than 20 C and mortalities can be as high as 50%. (Robinson and Meyer 1973). Morbidity may reach as high as 100%, but not all species of fish present in an affected pond may be susceptible (Neish, 1980; Post, 1987). The course of infection is usually rapid and is exacerbated by crowding, algal blooms, or increased levels of un-ionized ammonia.

[4.2.3] ICTHYOPHONUS DISEASE (SWINGING DISEASE)

This disease is caused by a fungus, named *Icthyophonus hoferi*. It grows in fresh and saltwater, in wild and cultured fish, but is restricted to cool temperatures (36-68°F). The disease is spread by fungal cysts, that are discharged into the faeces, and by cannibalism of infected fish. As the principal mechanism of transmission is through the ingestion of infected spores, there are no visible signs of this disease in fish with a mild to moderate infection. In severe conditions, the skin may have a texture like sandpaper caused by skin and muscle infection. Some fish may show the curvature of the spine. Internally, the organs may be swollen with white to grey-white sores. Diseased fish show curious swinging movements, hence the disease is called "swinging disease". Along with the liver, particularly severely affected organs are: the spleen (in salmonids), the heart (in herring), the kidney (in salmonids), the gonads, the brain (in salmonids), the gills (in salmonids), and the muscles and nerve tissue behind the eyes (in sea fish) (Klinger, 1996).

[4.2.4] OTHER FUNGAL DISEASES

The three fungal diseases described above are the most commonly encountered. There are, however, other fungi that have been implicated in fish diseases. Some of the genera involved include *AspergIllus* (Olufemi, 1983; Bhattacharya, 1995), *Aureobasidum* (Otte, 1964), *Candida* (Neish, 1980; Hatai, 1975), *Cryptococcus* (Pierotti, 1971), *Exophilia* (McGinnis, 1974; Langdon, 1987), *Fusarium* (Crow, 1995), *Hormoconis* (Strongman, 1997), *Paecilomyces* (Lightner, 1988), *Phoma* (Hatai, 1986), *Phialophora* (Ellis et al., 1983), *Ochroconis* (*Scolocobasidium*), (Schaumann, 1994; Wada, 1995; Ross, 1973; Ajello et al., 1977; McGinnis, 1974; Doty, 1946) and *Rhizomucor* (Wolf, 1999). Most of these are single-or multiple-case reports, and the fungi involved in most instances have been known to cause systemic disease in fish. In the past, some have also included *Ichthyophonus hoferi* as well as *Dermocystidium* in the discussions on fungal diseases of fish. Although both have fungal-like elements, recent reports have suggested that both *Ichthyophonus* and *Dermocystidium* belong to a clade of unnamed protistians (Ragan, 1996; Spangguard, 1996) and they were not included in this review.

[4.3] DIAGNOSIS OF FUNGAL DISEASES

Diagnosis is a medical condition in which a disease is recognized using various diagnostic approaches based on its symptoms and signs. This diagnosis helps the researcher to recognize a disease based on its most obvious symptoms, as well as analyze the disease's physiological and biochemical causes. A diagnosis process for analyzing the cause and nature of a disease is called disease diagnosis. Proper diagnosis helps in the proper treatment of disease and prevents the use of various chemotherapeutics.

One of the very first methods of disease diagnosis is by eye observation. Without any proper equipment or instruments, we can just observe various symptoms and signs of disease through our eyes. This foremost method used in disease diagnosis was proper case history information, which helps to know the cause of disease development. Some of the methods used in this literature were to check water quality, feeding percentage, swimming behavior, stocking details, etc. These are the fundamental processes for disease diagnosis to know the nature of the disease and how it developed.

Previous researchers used some of the equipment for fish disease diagnosis. One of the most important pieces of equipment was a high-quality microscope with 10X, 40X, and 100X objective lenses. Simple surgical instruments such as scalpels, fine and coarse scissors, fine and coarse forceps, disposable gloves, and a 10% formalin solution were among the other necessities. Clean 30–40 liters of water, plastic buckets, various-sized aquarium bags, and an aquarium container with a small air pump were also necessary (available from a local aquarium shop).

Identification of infected fish was previously done by many researchers with the help of (Jhingran, 1991). To protect fish from disease and parasites, fish have a number of defenses. The current review focuses on bacterial diseases, viral diseases, and fungal diseases, among other types of freshwater fish diseases. For a different types of disease, a different type of treatment will be needed.

In most cases, fungal disease appears as a thin, cottony (floccous) white growth on the skin, gills, or on fish eggs when in water. The color of these lesions often varies because the mycelium tends to entrap sediment particles or algae and may appear to be red, brown, or green. Out of the water, the floccous appearance is difficult to perceive because the mycelium collapses into a slimy, matted mass. Initial lesions are often focal, small, and inconspicuous, but they can rapidly enlarge because of the rapid development of the mycelium over a short period of time. The scales of the fish are frequently evaluated from the body if the infection is on a scaled surface. Although superficial (epidermal) initially, these lesions may extend into the dermis and the subjacent superficial musculature with time.

These early lesions are usually pale with a ring of erythema surrounding them. Sloughing of the epidermis ensues. As a result, chronic infections invariably result in erosions or superficial ulcerations, which in most instances, are covered by the fungal mat. Some saprolegnian infections have been reported to spread from the gills to the pharynx and oesophagus (Bruno and Stamps, 1987), while others have been known to infect other tissues, including the liver, spleen, kidney, swim bladder, eye, and brain (Bruno and Stamps, 1987). (Neish, 1980; Egusa, 1991; Wolke, 1975). Indeed, some of the saprolegnian fungi have the gastrointestinal tract as the initial site of infection (Miyazaki et al., 1977) and, experimentally, some of these infections are limited to the internal organs (Yuasa and Hati, 1995).

A tentative diagnosis is based on microscopic examination of skin scrapes or gill clips of the lesions of a live or fleshly dead fish (moribund when collected). This is a necessity because of the ubiquitous nature of these organisms, and dead fish can be rapidly colonized because they make excellent substrates. Microscopically, there is usually regionally extensive dermal necrosis, hemorrhage, edema, and myocyte necrosis. Because of the extent of the lesions, death as a result of saprolegniasis, in most cases, can be attributed to loss of osmoregulatory ability.

[4.4] TREATMENT OF FUNGAL DISEASE

Saprolegniasis is best prevented by good management practices, such as good water quality and circulation, avoidance of crowding to minimize injury (especially during spawning), and good nutrition. Once Saprolegnia is identified in an aquatic system, sanitation should be evaluated and corrected. Common treatments include potassium permanganate, formalin and povidone iodine solutions. Over treatment can further damage fish tissue, resulting in recurring infections. Environmental management is essential for satisfactory resolution of chronic problems. Bath treatment in NaOH (10-25 g/L for 10-20 min), KmNO4 (1 g in 100 L of water for 30-90 min) or in CuSO4 (5-10 g in 100 L of water for 10-30 min) should be done.

Avoidance is the best control for branchiomycosis. Good management techniques will create an environmental condition that is unfavorable for fungus growth. If the disease is present, the sick fish should not be transported. Great care must be taken to prevent the movement of the disease to non-infected areas. Formalin and copper sulphate have been used to help stop mortalities. All tanks, raceways, and aquaria, on the other hand, must be disinfected and dried. Ponds should be dried and treated with quicklime (calcium oxide). This problem can be improved by taking a 7-day bath in Acriflavine Neutral or Forma-Green. Quicklime (calcium oxide) and copper sulphate (2-3 kg/ha) should be used to dry ponds.

Fish that have died from infection, should be buried. Fish infected with *Icthyophonus hoferi* do not have a cure; they will carry the infection for the rest of their lives. The only way to keep things under control is to prevent them from happening in the first place. Never feed raw fish or raw fish items to farmed fish to avoid the introduction of infectious spores. Cooking helps destroy the infective life stage. Once icthyophonus disease is identified by a trained diagnostician, the infected fish should be removed and destroyed. Complete disinfection of tanks, raceways, or aquaria is encouraged. Ponds with dirt or gravel bottoms need drying to totally eliminate the fungus (Wolf, 1988).

As alluded to above, there are usually one or more predisposing factors that allow for saprolengniasis. Temperature plays a significant role, with the majority of epizootics present at lower temperatures (Roberts, 1989; Bly et al., 1993). However, while saprolegniasis can occur at higher temperatures (Roberts, 1989) and coldwater fish are more resistant to infection at lower temperatures, because coldwater fish are more resistant to infection at lower temperatures (Neish, 1980). In channel catfish, the rapid decrease in water temperature results in the loss of protective mucus from the epidermis (Quiniou et al., 1998) and increases susceptibility to saprolegniasis. Elevated steroid hormones (eg, cortisol and androgens) can reduce the number of mucus cells (Noga, 1993). Aside from affecting mucus cell numbers, cortisol can also increase susceptibility by affecting inflammatory responses and ascorbic acid metabolism (Neish, 1980).

Trauma, overhandling, and other unfavorable environmental factors (e.g., increased nitrogenous waste, low pH stress) can all cause saprolegniasis in fish. Because there is usually only limited success with treatments, minimizing these predisposing factors is integral to controlling saprolegniasis. This is also true of fungal infections in hatcheries, (Francis-Floyd, 1994), where a range of Oomycete infections have been reported (Kitancharoen et al., 1997). Only dead eggs are usually infected, and the disease then spreads to the adjacent living eggs, (Neish, 1980), most likely through the release of fungal enzymes (Rand and Munden, 1992). In order to reduce fungal infections in hatcheries, it is necessary to remove dead or infertile eggs, maintain good hygiene, and maintain proper water quality and temperature (Tucker and Robinson, 1990).

Although not a treatment, quarantine is an important feature in the management of fish infections. As a general rule, if possible, for at least 1-week, new introductions to a system should be housed separately. Those that have become diseased should also be quarantined to minimize spread and to facilitate treatments. Further details are available in some of the references (Egusa, 1991; Srivasta, 1987; Post, 1987; Noga, 1996; Stoskopf, 1993). Zinc-free malachite green has been considered the quint essential antifungal agent for treating fish and fish eggs (Egusa, 1991; Srivasta, 1987; Post, 1987; Noga, 1993; Willoughby and Roberts, 1992).

It is not approved for food fish because of its teratogenic, mutagenic, and carcinogenic effects (Neish, 1980; Noga, 1993). Some have used formalin together with green malachite because formalin is not efficient on its own (Post, 1987; Noga, 1993). However, formalin is the only approved drug for use in food fish that is efficacious, at least experimentally (Meng et al., 1996; Federal joint, 1994). Formalin will chemically lower the dissolved oxygen of the water and can also adversely affect the dissolved oxygen because it is toxic to algae as well as for plants.

When formalin is stored at lower temperatures and exposed to light, it can include paraformaldehyde precipitates, which are highly hazardous to fish. The water molds are sensitive to salt (which may be the reason why marine fish species are not susceptible to saprolegnian infections), and hence salt baths have been used in treating the disease and as a prophylactic therapeutant (Neish, 1980; Noga, 1993).

However, salt has been proven to be useless as a preventive treatment in some cases, particularly in commercial aquaculture, because relatively very high concentrations are required for successful treatment (Meng et al., 1996; Federal joint, 1994). Treatments for saprolegniasis have included acetic acid, methylene blue, and hydrogen peroxide (Srivasta, 1987; Post, 1987; Noga, 1993; Khoo et al., 1998). Despite the fact that a list of therapies isn't totally satisfactory, novel biological controls are also being explored (Neish, 1980). Prevention by means of good husbandry and maintaining water quality are keys to preventing this disease. The primary problem should also be addressed if saprolegniasis is secondary.

For the treatment of branchiomycosis, several chemicals have been suggested. Malachite green (0.3 mg/L for a 24-hour bath), benzalkonium chloride (1 to 4 ppm, 1-hour dip), copper sulphate (100 rag/L, 10-to 30-minute dip), formalin (15 ppm at first, then 25 ppm), and feeding methylene blue are a few examples (Neish, 1980; Srivasta, 1987; Post, 1987). However, these treatment protocols and their efficacy are not well established, hence there is no one recommended treatment (Neish, 1980). The disease also has an acute onset and rapid progression, which makes prevention rather than treatment the key to controlling this disease. Prophylactic methods such as quick lime (to raise the pH and purify the water) and copper sulphate have been advised to prevent recurrence. Improving water quality (e.g., by reducing feeding and stocking density) may also be important in the disease's prevention and treatment. During the epizootic stage, removing dead fish is also critical for lowering the source point of infection. Hydrogen peroxide has the potential to be used as a fungicidal treatment against this infection (Lilley, 1997). Vaccinations against this fungus are also being explored (Thompson et al., 1999).

[4.5] SUMMARY

The table and figure given below summarises all fungal diseases, including symptoms and causal microorganisms.

Table 2. Fungal disease

Sl No	Disease Condition	Symptoms	Involvement of Pathogens
1	Saprolegniasis	Fish become weak, ulceration of skin with haemorrhages, cotton wool growth on ulcers with grey patches	*Saprolegnia parasitica*
2	Branchiomycosis (Gill rot disease)	Fish become lethargic, redness of gills, which later become greyish-white, necrosis of gill filaments	*Branchiomyces demigrans.*
3	Icthyophonus Disease (Swinging Disease)	fish starts to show swinging movement.	*Icthyophonus hoferi*

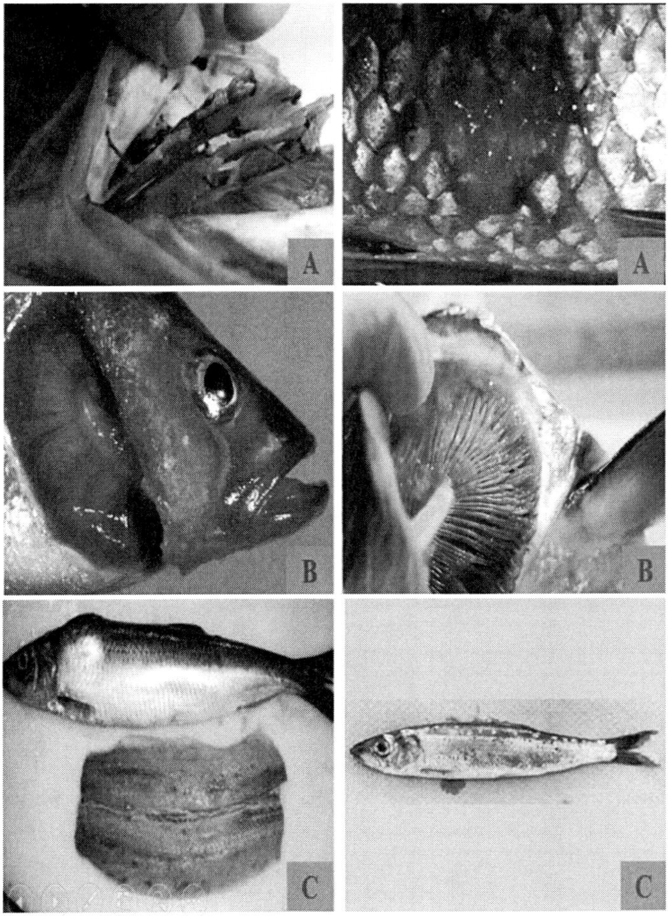

Figure 2. Fungal diseases, (A) Saprolegniasis, (B) Branchiomycosis, (C) Icthyophonus Disease

VIRAL DISEASES

[5.1] INTRODUCTION OF VIRAL DISEASES

Viruses, unlike bacteria, exist as particles with no nucleus, organelle, or metabolic system. A virion is the name of a virus particle. For replication, it is dependent on the synthesizing structure of the host cells. As a result, viruses are obligatory pathogens. Viruses that cause disease are either spherical or rod-shaped. All other groups are referred to as complex or binal viruses. Viruses are classified on the basis of the type of nucleic acid in the virion (Bassey, 2011).

Cell culture techniques are used to isolate and identify the pathogens of fish viruses. Cytopathic effects caused on cultured cells and serum neutralization techniques. In fish, there is no antibiotic or chemotherapeutic drug that can treat or control viral disease. Effective control procedures include testing and slaughter, quarantine, movement restrictions, cleanliness, and disinfection. Vaccines can help to control a variety of viral infections in larger vertebrates, but they are rarely effective in fish (Bassey, 2011).

The absence of active virological research in India restricts our knowledge of viral infection to those detectable by externally visible or microscopically recognizable virus-induced pathological changes. Lymphocystis infection in cichlids from East African lakes (Paperna, 1973) is the only confirmed case of viral infection in African fish.

A case of mortality, with characteristic abdominal dropsy of carp, in Kajansi farm, Uganda, could have been associated with viral (*Rhabdovirus carpio*) aetiology. The rhabdovirus caused carp disease (SVC) occurs predominantly in coldwater regions, although in cell culture the virus was found to grow in temperatures up to 31°C (Fijan et al., 1971).

Avtalion and Shlapobersky (1994) described a whirling viral disease in tilapia fry that caused mortalities of laboratory reared (less than one monthold) *Oreochromis aureus, O. niloticus, Sarotherodon galilaeus*, and *tilapia* hybrids, including red tilapia. Prior to death, the affected fish were dark-skinned, anorexic, and exhibited typical whirling behaviour. The first signs of disease appeared in 4–8-day-old fish. Death appeared first in 6–8-day old fish and, subsequently, another wave in 14–18-day old fish. Hexagonal particles, iridovirus-like, of about 100 nm, were demonstrated within inclusions in the endoplasmic reticulum in cells from brain tissue.

The Herpes-like infections of the nuclei and cytoplasm of haematopoietic kidney cells were demonstrated in pond reared goldfish from Israel, which also showed severe infection of the same tissue by gram negative bacteria (apparently *Aeromonas salmonicida*). The highly contagious herpes virus, which causes disease in cultivated American catfish (CCV) in the Southern United States, has been shown to be transmissible and pathogenic to *Clarias batranchus*, posing a potential epizootic risk to catfish (siluroids) if introduced into Africa with its American catfish host. Cusack and Cone (1986) evaluated data that suggested parasitic crustaceans could be vectors for fish virus infections.

Neoplasia and degenerative chronic conditions are often linked to anthropogenic stresses on the ecosystem, in particular due to the release of xenobiotic materials into the environment (Edwards and Overstreet, 1976; Hawkins et al., 1988). These conditions are less visible in less developed areas, and while they may exist in some places, relevant documentation is presently absent. Certain fish diseases do not have any known causes. Environmental diseases result from inadequacies in the physical and chemical characteristics of water. Ingestion of feed proteins containing hazardous amino acids can cause nutritional problems.

In this review section of the viral diseases: Virus Hemorrhagic Septicemia, and Carp Spring Viraemia (CSV) fish diseases were explained briefly. More than 125 distinct viruses have been detected in fish from all over the world, and new viruses are discovered every day. In India, however, there have been few reports of viral infections affecting finfish. In ornamental fish culture, Cyprinid Herpesvius-2 (CyHV-2), Koi Rana Viral (KIRV), Carp Edema

Virus (CEV), Megalocytiviris, and Goldfish haematopoietic virus necrosis herpes have all been reported (Sahoo et al., 2013). In the ornamental fishery, KIRV has been found to cause massive mortality in koi *Cyprinus carpio*. In addition, CEV-induced koi sleepiness has been recorded in *Cyprinus carpio* (Swaminathan et al., 2016). A Report of Viral Encephalopathy and Retinopathy (VER) or Betanoda virus was also reported for a period in seabass farming, although there were no subsequent reports of such disease occurrences in India.

The pattern of disease occurrence and mortality is typical in the Indian aquaculture system. While the occurrence of viral diseases, especially White spot disease, has caused havoc in shrimp aquaculture, viral disease outbreaks have not been the cause of concern in fish culture. The significant observation is that so far there has not been a single case of viral disease outbreak has been reported in freshwater aquaculture in India, causing huge mortality. It may be that India is blessed with an Indigenous Variety of Indian Major Carps (IMCS) which are not susceptible to fish viral pathogens as prevalent in other Asian countries, or that the cultural environment is not conducive for the viral pathogens to multiply and cause disease.

However, parasite infestations in fish culture have been a source of concern, as they are responsible for a higher rate of morbidity and productivity loss than other pathogens. In freshwater aquaculture, parasite infestations are the most common (46 percent), followed by losses due to changes in water quality factors (24 percent), both of which result in production losses. Infection of fish with bacterial pathogens is in the range of 22% and in only 8% of cases is mortality due to other factors (Wolf, 1988).

Virus infections that affect warm-water fish in both the freshwater and marine environment. Freshwater fish account for the majority of global aquaculture production and a significant part of the inland catch-fish business (FAO, 2007). The harvest of farmed warm water fish is increasing due to financial investment and refinement in technologies and a continuous increase in cultivated species. The production of fish species for aquaculture has also increased rapidly, and disease problems have become the largest obstacle to aquaculture operations. Furthermore, some diseases of cultured fish have currently spread to wild populations of fish (e.g., koi herpesvirus disease; Haenen and Hedrick, 2006).

Wolf (1988) described 59 fish viruses and fish viral diseases and, subsequent to that review, the number of known fish viruses has surpassed 100 and continues to increase (Fijan, 1999). The diseases mentioned in this chapter are transboundary aquatic animal diseases that are currently of international concern due to their socioeconomic impact within affected countries and their significance in the international trade of aquatic animals and aquatic animal products. The World Organization for Animal Health has a list of most of the diseases described (OIE, 2006; 2009a). Viruses that cause only a few infections in cultured animals, viruses with poor virulence or those that cause hyperplastic lesions in feral fish, and viruses that have only been reported once are not discussed.

[5.2] TYPES OF VIRAL DISEASES

[5.2.1] CARP SPRING VIRAEMIA (CSV)

This is an acute to chronic viral disease that affects a variety of carp species. During the rainy season, when the pond water temperature begins to rise, most epizootics of this disease occur. This disease is also known to occur during the winter months of the year. The *Rhabdo* virus causes the condition. The *Rhabdo* virus is the cause of the disease. Hemorrhage on the skin and around the anus, belly swelling, paleness of the gills, and, in chronic cases, ulcerative hemorrhagic dermatitis and widespread odema are all indications of the condition. Internal symptoms include a large amount of serum or blood-tinged fluid in the abdomen, a pale or hemorrhagic liver, necrotic muscular tissues, and hemorrhages on the surface of the swim bladder, intestine, kidney, and spleen. Diagnostic procedures include isolation and identification of the virus by histopathology and the use of clinical signs. Treatment is unknown, however quarantine, restriction of contaminated fish migration, and proper cleanliness can help reduce the disease.

Spring viraemia of carp (SVC) is an acute, systemic, contagious disease caused by a rhabdovirus (Bootsma and Ebregt, 1983; Wolf, 1988; Ahne et al., 2002). The term SVC The name Rhabdovirus carpio (RVC) for the causal agent was introduced by Fijan et al. (1971). This disease is mostly found in common carp. Several additional species of cyprinids and a few other cyprinids are also susceptible. SVC is most common in the spring, when the water temperature is below 18°C.

SVC was previously classified as part of the condition known as infectious dropsy of carp (IDC) or infectious ascites, hemorrhagic septicemia, red contagious sickness, or rubella, until it was identified as a separate aetiological and clinical entity. Initially, IDC was thought to be a bacterial infection. Because mixed infections with bacteria are widespread in fish, the distinction between two types of IDC, acute or ascitic and chronic or ulcerative, is to some extent a point of controversy. Tomasec et al. (1964) and Osadcaja (1964) identified cytopathic agents from IDC, which could have been spring viraemia of carp virus (SVCV). IDC and its synonyms, according to

Fijan (1972), covered a variety of aetiological and pathological phenomena. SVC was clearly included in the acute or ascitic form of IDC, and some chronic IDC matched carp erythrodermatitis produced by a typical *Aeromonas salmonicida* (Fijan, 1972; Bootsma et al., 1977; Fijan, 1999). IDC also included information on swim-bladder inflammation (SBI), *Pseudomonas fluorescens* infection, motile aeromonad infection, and some cases of columnaris illness with skin lesions.

Spring viraemia of carp virus (SVCV), also known as *Rhabdovirus carpio* (RVC), is currently classified as a species in the genus *Vesiculovirus* of the family Rhabdoviridae (order Mononegavirales) according to the (Hoffmann et al., 2005; Kuzmin et al., 2009). The aetiological role of RVC in SVC was confirmed by Baudouy (1975), Rudikov et al. (1975), Ahne (1977), Hill (1977), Tesarckk et al. (1977), Békési and Szabó (1979), Bucke and Finlay (1979). Ahne (1976) and Bachmann and Ahne (1973, 74). The virus caused bleeding and inflammation of the swim bladder, which is a common clinical symptom of the disease.

Some studies have shown some possibility that virus-specific neutralizing antibodies in fish serum could be used to diagnose SVC infection (Sulimanovic, 1973; Kölbl and Kainz, 1977; Wizigmann et al., 1980, 1983; Dixon et al., 1994).

However, due to lack of information of the serological responses of fish to virus infections, the detection of specific antibodies to viruses has not been accepted thus far as a routine screening method for assessing the viral status of fish populations (OIE,2006).

[5.2.2] VIRAL HEMORRHAGIC SEPTICEMIA VIRUS (VHSV)

VHS (viral hemorrhagic septicemia) is one of the most important viral fish diseases in India, as well as of salmonid fish in European aquaculture (Olesen 1998), causing annual losses of $40 million pounds in 1991 (Hill 1992). Arhabdo viruses produce this viral disease, which can be acute or chronic. Infected fish excrete virus particles in their urine and on their faces. As a result, the disease is spread by contact with contaminated water. The incubation period of the disease is between ten and fifteen days. Except for the occurrence of cutaneous inflammation in virus hemorrhagic septicemia, the signs and autopsies of the disease are identical to those of infectious hematopoietic necrosis.

Hemorrhages in muscle tissue, liver, viscera fat, gonads, and other organs are also some noticeable similarities at autopsy. The liver becomes pale or yellowish in colour. When it is chronic, the kidneys and spleen swell. The symptoms, histology, isolation and identification of the virus pathogen can all be used to diagnose this disease. There is no proper therapeutic treatment for this condition. Prevention is through quarantine and restriction of fish suspected to be infected, strict sanitation of hatchery facilities, and testing and slaughter methods.

VHS is caused by the Egtved virus, also known as viral haemorrhagic septicaemia virus, which is a negative-stranded RNA virus (VHSV). The virus is a member of the Rhabdoviridae family and belongs to the newly recognized *Novirhabdovirus* genus (Walker et al., 2000). The virus is enveloped and has a genome of 11–12 kilobase nucleotides that codes for five structural proteins.

The rainbow trout is the most vulnerable fish species by this disease. The disease causes hemorrhages in the meninges, serous surfaces, muscles, internal organs, and in the eyes, as well as exophthalmia, body darkening, and pale gills in farmed rainbow trout. Ascites can be seen on occasion. The damaged fish are sluggish and lethargic. Dark discoloration and altered swimming behaviour might be seen in the chronic stages (Wolf 1988). Mortality varies depending on the age of the fish, but it can be as high as 100% in fry, however it is usually lower in older fish, ranging from 30% to 70%.

Clinically infected fish and covert carriers among farmed, feral, and wild fish serve as VHSV reservoirs. Urine and ovarian fluids shed the pathogenic virus. Viruses are most prevalent in the kidney and spleen (Wolf, 1988), and these organs are also the target organs in rainbow trout (Brudeseth et al., 2002). Because of latent viral carrier fish, once VHSV is established in a farmed stock and, thus, in a water catchment system, the disease becomes enzootic.

The widespread presence of VHSV in wild marine fish species in northern Europe raises questions regarding VHS's status in coastal zones, which may have implications for member states requesting VHS-free status in coastal zones and inland water systems. Diadromous fish migrate upstream into freshwater, posing a risk of VHSV transmission into rainbow trout farms.

In both natural disease cases and infection trials, variations in virus strain virulence have been observed, however the subtyping approach is unable to distinguish between strains of varying virulence. Nor can it discriminate between marine strains that aren't pathogenic to rainbow trout and farmed strains that are pathogenic to rainbow trout (Skall et al., 2004). The development of diagnostic procedures for typing VHSV isolates according to pathogenicity and geographical origin will be critical in adjusting EC disease regulations to account for the unexpected occurrence of VHSV in the marine environment.

[5.3] DIAGNOSIS OF VIRAL DISEASES

Diagnosis is a medical condition in which a disease is identified by its symptoms and signs by using various diagnostic methods. disease diagnosis is a procedure, that is used to identify the cause and nature of any disease. Proper diagnosis of disease is very important for providing the proper treatment and avoiding unnecessary chemotherapeutics uses. One of the very first step of disease diagnosis is eye observation. Various signs and symptoms of infections can be clearly seen with the help of eyes, without any proper diagnostic method. Some of the methods used by previous researchers on this review have been to test water quality, feeding percentage, swimming behavior, stocking details, etc. These are the primary methods for disease analysis to recognize the nature of the disease and how it developed.

The clinical signs of SVC are non-specific, and not all fish will exhibit all of the signs. Initially, there may be increasing mortality, often with a rapid onset. Infected fish may swim slowly and erratically, lose balance and swim on their sides. Two of the most obvious and consistent features are abdominal distension and hemorrhages. The latter may occur on the skin, fin bases, eyes, and gills, which may be pale. The skin may darken and exophthalmia is often observed. The vent may be swollen, inflamed, and trail mucoid casts. The abdomen is usually filled with a clear fluid, sometimes bloodstained. The spleen is often enlarged, most internal organs are usually oedematous, and organs adhere to each other and to the peritoneum. There are petechial hemorrhages in the muscles and the bladder (Dixon, 2008), though these are uncommon in SVC caused by Asian strains of SVCV (Goodwin, 2003; Dikkeboom et al., 2004).

Gaafar et al. (2011) conducted a detailed histopathological study on common carp and compared their findings with those of other authors, and Misk et al. (2016) recently reported the histopathology of SVC in three experimental hosts. Histopathological studies commonly reveal oedema, inflammation, hemorrhage, and necrosis in the liver, pancreas, intestine, spleen, kidney, heart, muscles, and air bladder, but again, not all fish will exhibit each feature.

A definitive diagnosis of SVC is made by isolation of the virus in cell culture followed by its identification using serological and molecular methods. The OIE, in its Manual of Diagnostic Tests for Aquatic Animals, includes comprehensive methodology to diagnose and identify SVC (OIE, 2015a). Mortality of fingerlings and older fish can be expected at temperatures below 18–20°C, i.e., in the spring and at the beginning of the summer, but less frequently in the autumn and winter.

Behavioral, external, and internal symptoms are used to make a clinical diagnosis. The disease symptoms listed here are based on uncomplicated natural SVC outbreaks and laboratory experiments (Fijan et al., 1971; Fijan, 1972, 1973, 1975; Bachmann and Ahne, 1973, 1974). Fish that are terminally lethargic, swim on their side, move slowly, or rest in a normal or aberrant position gather around pond banks in the early stage of infection. Exophthalmos, petechial hemorrhage, and ecchymoses in the skin, gills, and anterior eye chamber, anemia and pale gills, as well as protrusion and inflammation of the vent are all external symptoms of SVC. Shedding of long, white to yellowish, thick mucoid casts from the vent is readily visible in fish kept in experimental facilities.

Oedema in all organs, hemorrhage, peritonitis, and catarrhal enteritis are the most common internal symptoms. Hemorrhage can occur in little to large amounts of transparent fluid in the peritoneal cavity. Fibrinous peritonitis causes organs to adhere to each other and to the parietal peritoneum. Internal organs and muscles show signs of Petechial bleeding. Hemorrhage is easily recognizable in the lamina epithelial is of the swim bladder. The spleen is enlarged, and hemorrhagic or ischemic infarcts might occur.

Specific diagnosis of SVC is based generally on the isolation of SVCV in cell culture, followed by its immunological or nucleic acid-based identification, such as PCR (OIE, 2006). Isolation of the virus in cell culture is the most sensitive and widely used approach. Identification of SVCV antigen in tissues of moribund and dead infected carp is possible using IFAT (Faisal and Ahne, 1984) and ELISA on tissue extracts (Way, 1991; Rodak et al., 1993). PCR-based methods are preferred for SVC diagnosis because of their high specificity and convenience. A reverse transcription (RT)-PCR protocol described by OIE (2006) can amplify the partial G gene of both SVCV and PFRV and, therefore, subsequent sequencing of the amplicon has to be carried out for identification. Furthermore, the SVCV subgroup can be identified using a BLAST search of the sequence data.

A virus isolated in cell culture must be identified, but some antisera cross-react with other viruses, such as pike fry rhabdovirus (PFRV). Antisera may also react with some isolates and not others (Dixon, 2008). Hence, definitive identification of SVCV in culture is best achieved by using RT-PCR based methods. The assay adopted by the OIE targets a partial nucleotide sequence of the G gene of a wide range of SVCV isolates and other closely related viral isolates that could be misidentified as SVCV serologically (Stone et al., 2003). According to Stone et al. (2003), there are four genogroups: genogroup I comprise SVCV isolates, genogroup II is a single isolate from grass carp, genogroup III comprises the reference PFRV isolate, and genogroup IV, also called the tench rhabdovirus group, comprises unassigned isolates and isolates previously identified as PFRV. However, the International Committee for Taxonomy of Viruses (ICTV) recognizes only two species, SVCV and PFRV, with the grass carp rhabdovirus and tench rhabdovirus considered to belong within the PFRV species (Adams et al., 2014).

The pathophysiology of SVC is not well studied. What is known was derived from studies of natural infections and from one experimental infection. Rehulka (1996) studied the development of SVC in carp that had been taken from a State Fishery overwintering pond and found them to be susceptible to SVC at the end of their hibernation. In diseased carp (as confirmed by virus isolation and neutralization), there was a decrease in lymphocytes, an increase in neutrophils, particularly myelocytes and metamyelocytes, and an increase in monocytes.

These changes were associated with the worsening health of the fish and were accompanied by a change in the morphology of the cells, particularly vacuolization of the nucleus and cytoplasm. There were also indications of anemia. Overall, the disease caused almost 60% mortality. During the course of the disease, Osadchaya and Rudenko (1981) reported a marked decrease in glycogen synthesis in the liver as indicated by a practically complete absence of glycogen granules in hepatocytes and a very small quantity of iron-containing pigment in the splenic pulp. According to Fijan (1999), the multiplication of SVCV in the capillary epithelium and in hematopoietic and excretory kidney tissues affects osmoregulation, which could be fatal.

In acute cases of branchiomycosis, the gills have a marbled appearance because of the hemorrhage and infected tissue. Blood flow in the vessels is blocked by the fungus mycelia, causing thrombosis. This corresponds to the dark red-brown areas in the gills, which contrasts with the light grayish-white ischemic zones. Fungal hyphae, sometimes light brown, slightly refractory, branched, and nonseptate on gill-wet mountings, frequently exist in the gill vessels and in particular, in the base of the primary lamellae and the gill arch. There is usually mild to moderate swelling and hemorrhage of the branchial tissue with obliteration of the interlamellar troughs (Khoo et al., 1998).

These fungi have broad hyphae (approximately 8 to 35 m), which most often contain granular spores that are approximately 5 to 17 m in diameter (Srivasta, 1987; Post, 1987). Special stains (GMS and PAS) can also be used to highlight the fungus in histological sections. As with saprolegniasis, there is usually no inflammatory infiltrate associated with the fungus, especially if it remains within the vessels. However, a moderate to noticeable granulomatous infiltration may sometimes occur, particularly if the fungus exists a vessel (Khoo et al., 1998).

[5.4] TREATMENT OF VIRAL DISEASE

Both the prevention and control of SVC are currently enacted through legislation and good management. Prevention has also been attempted by vaccination and the use of resistant strains of carp. For example, Kirpichnikov et al. (1993) reported that the hybrid line of Ukrainian-Ropsha carp had increased resistance to SVC compared with other stocks or strains of carp. Commercial vaccines underwent field trials in the former Czechoslovakia in the 1970s and 1980s (Fijan, 1984, 1988; Dixon, 1997; Sano et al., 2011). However, the vaccine is no longer available, and problems with interpretation of the trials have been discussed by Dixon (1997).

Oral vaccination using low virulence SVCV, or virus attenuated by passage through cell cultures, has been attempted. Laboratory experiments showed promise, but a large-scale field trial with pond-cultured fish was unsuccessful (Fijan, 1988). Oral vaccination utilizing different attenuated viruses was also investigated (Kolbl, 1980). Survival in field trials was encouraging (15% mortality in vaccinated fish versus 49% mortality in control fish). The vaccine was modified by an unspecified method and vaccination in the field was successful as judged by no SVC being observed along with an increase in yield. For example, there was an increase from a low yield of 15 t at one site, which was attributed to SVC, to 50 t in the first year following vaccination, and to 70 t the year after. The vaccine did not go on to be commercialized.

Different approaches to vaccine production have subsequently been undertaken, but none has produced a commercial vaccine. Recombinant SVCV glycoprotein injected into carp produced neutralizing antibodies but did not protect fish against SVCV (Dixon, 1997). A genetically engineered Lactobacillus plantarum with a surface-expressing SVCV glycoprotein and cyprinid herpesvirus-3 (CyHV-3) ORF81 protein was incorporated into pelleted feed as an oral vaccine (Cui et al., 2015). Under experimental conditions, there was 29% mortality in vaccinated carp compared with 78 and 89% mortality in control fish challenged with SVCV. The vaccine also protected koi carp against CyHV-3. There have been laboratory trials with DNA vaccines based on the G gene of SVCV. Different combinations of SVCV DNA plasmids containing partial or complete G gene fragments were compared (Kanellos et al., 2006). Two vaccinated groups of common carp had relative percentage survival (RPS) values of 33 and 48% in challenges that produced > 60% mortality in control fish. Shivappa et al., (2008) used a single DNA vaccine to immunize koi carp against SVCV and the RPS ranged from 50 to 70%.

Interferon-inducer double-stranded RNA injected into carp prior to challenge with SVCV reduced mortality from 100% to 22–40% (Alikin et al., 1996). The use of liposomes containing poly (I:C) (polyinosinic–polycytidylic acid, a synthetic interferon inducer) and bacterial lipopolysaccharide as an immunostimulant prior to SVCV infection has also been investigated. The administration of the liposomes to zebrafish by immersion or IP injection reduced mortality (RPS of 33.3 and 42.3%, respectively) following challenge. Methisoprinol (an antiviral agent) inhibited the replication of SVCV in vitro, but its efficacy was not tested in fish (Siwicki et al., 2003).

Without commercial vaccines or therapeutic substances, biosecurity strategies remain the most effective way of preventing SVC. These range from national or international legislation or standards to good management practices at the farm level. The latter include on-site quarantine of new fish stocks, the disinfection of equipment, the use of footbaths, and reducing stress and other diseases, etc. Several studies have identified disinfectants and other chemical or physical means for inactivating the virus (Kiryu et al., 2007; Dixon, 2008; Dixon et al., 2012), although the results from these studies must be interpreted with care. For example, 99.9% of SVCV was inactivated in hydrochloric acid after 2 h at pH 3.0 (Ahne, 1976), but in formic acid at pH 4.0 (to mimic the procedure used to dispose of dead fish), the virus survived for at least 28 days (Dixon et al., 2012).

Legislation to control the introduction and spread of diseases within a country is the most important way of preventing and controlling SVC. Such legislation is often strengthened by international standards or agreements. The OIE's Aquatic Animal Health Code (OIE, 2015b) outlines approaches to biosecurity that can be implemented from the national level down to a production site. Hastein et al., (2008), have outlined an overview of the implementation of biosecurity strategies, which uses SVC as a diseas- specific case study. Oidtmann et al., (2011), reviewed the international standards relating to the movement of fish and fish products, particularly with emphasis on national measures to combat fish disease. The UK has implemented a fish health strategy to establish freedom from SVC, which has been outlined by Taylor et al., (2013).

Legislative controls may have led to freedom from SVC in Croatia, and reduced the incidence of SVC in Hungary (Molnár and Csaba, 2005; Oraic and Zrncic, 2005). However, the epizootiology of the virus in individual countries will determine the feasibility of establishing an SVC free country. For example, SVC occurs predominantly in wild fish in the USA (Phelps et al., 2012), where establishing freedom from disease is difficult to achieve. Jeremic et al. (2004) were also pessimistic about an SVC-free Serbia because of repeated transfer of the disease from cultivated to wild carp and vice versa. However, even though SVC is widespread within a country, it may still be possible to establish disease-free zones, provided that fish movements are strictly controlled. Legislation to prevent the introduction of SVC via contaminated fish or fish products is an important approach. All movements, whether they involve live fish or processed contaminated products had been strictly controlled. Non-approved movements of such products may have introduced or reintroduced SVC into the USA and the UK (Hastein et al., 2008; Taylor et al., 2013). Therefore, continual surveillance of imported fish and fish products is essential.

[3.5] SUMMARY

The table and figure given below summarises all viral diseases, including symptoms and causal microorganisms.

Table 3. Viral diseases

S.no.	Disease Condition	Symptoms	Involveme nt of Pathogens
1	Carp spring viremia (CSV)	Lethargy; stay near tank bottom; awkward swimming	Rhabdovirus carpio
2	Viral Haemorrhagic septicemia virus (VHSV)	Anaemia; pale discolouration o gill; swelling of eyes and belly; odema of muscles; inflammation of intestine; anus become protruded.	Rhabdovirus

Figure 3. Viral diseases, (A) Carp spring viremia (B) Viral Haemorrhagic septicemia

REFERENCES

1. Abdul Kader Mydeen KP, Haniffa MA. (2011). Evaluation of antibacterial activity of medicinal plants on fish pathogen Aeromonas hydrophila. J Res Biol. 1:1-5.

2. Abell R., Blanch S., Revenga S. & Thieme M. (2009) Conservation of aquatic ecosystems. In: Encyclopedia of Inland Waters (Ed. G.E. Likens), pp. 249–258. Elsevier, Oxford, U.K.

3. Adams, M.J., Lefkowitz, E.J., King, A.M.Q. and Carstens, E.B. (2014) Ratification vote on taxonomic proposals to the International Committee on Taxonomy of Viruses (2014). Archives of Virology 159, 2831–2841

4. Ahne, W. (1976) Untersuchungen über die Stabilität des karpfenpathogenen Virusstammes 10/3. Fisch und Umwelt 2, 121–127

5. Ahne, W. (1977) Evidence for the systemic character of Rhabdovirus carpio infection. Bulletin de l'Offi ce International des Épizooties 1, 435–436.

6. Ahne, W., Bjorklund, H.V., Essbauer, S., Fijan, N., Kurath, G. and Winton, J.R. (2002) Spring viremia of carp (SVC). Diseases of Aquatic Organisms 52, 261–272.

7. Ainsworth G.C., An introduction to the history of mycology. London, Cambridge University Press, 1976

8. Ajello K, McGinnis MR, Camper J (1977) An outbreak of phaeohyphomycosis in rainbow trout caused by Scolecobasidium humicola. Mycopathologia 62:15-22.

9. Alderman DJ: Fungal disease of aquatic animals, in Roberts RJ (ed): Microbial Diseases of Fish. New York, Academic Press, 1982, pp 189-242

10. Altinok, I., & Kurt, I. (2003). Molecular diagnosis of fish diseases: a review. Turkish Journal of Fisheries and Aquatic Sciences, 3(2), 131-138.

11. American Veterinary Medical Association (2008) One health: a new professional imperative. One health initiative task force: final report. Available at: http:// www.avma.org/onehealth/default.asp

12. Anacker, R. L., and E. J. Ordal, 1955. Study of a bacteriophage infecting the myxobacterium Chondrococcus columnaris. J. Bacteriol. 70: 738-740.

13. Anderson, D.P., (1974). Fish Immunology. In: Diseases of fishes edited by Stanisias, F. Sneiszko, F. and Axelrod. H.R.F.H. Publication Inc. New Jersey 07753 USA.

14. Anderson, R. M. and May, R. M. Infectious diseases of humans. Oxford, UK: Oxford University Press. 1991

15. Anon 2009Aquaculture 2008. In Official statistics 4/2009 Helsinki, Finland: Finnish Game and Fisheries Research Institute.

16. Anon. (2017), Parasitic Diseases of Tilapia. 2017. www.thefishsite.com/articles/294/parasitic-diseases-of tilapia/ pp1-5.

17. Anonymous (1991) Council Directive 91/67/EEC of 28 January 1991 concerning the animal health conditions governing the placing on the market of aquaculture animals and products. Official Journal of the European Communities L046, 0001–0018.

18. Aoki T. Motile Aeromonads (Aeromonas hydrophila). In Fish Diseases and Disorders. Vol 3: Viral, Bacterial and Fungal Infections. Eds P. Woo, D. Bruno. Wallingford, CABI Publishing, 1999, 427-453 3.

19. Aquaticcommunity.com; 2011.

20. Ariel E. & Olesen N.J. (2002) Finfish in aquaculture and their diseases – a retrospective view on the European Community. Bulletin of the European Association of Fish Pathologists 22, 72–85.

21. Austin D. A. Bacterial Fish Pathogens, Disease of Farmed and Wild Fish, 4th Ed. Springer Praxis, Godalming, 2007.

22. Avtalion, R.R and M. Shlapobersky, (1994). A whirling viral disease of tilapia larvae. Israeli J. Aquacult. Bamidgeh, 46: 102-104.

23. Axelrod, H. R. Handbook of fish diseases. T.F.H. Publications, Neptune City, New Jersey. 1989

24. Bachmann, P.A. and Ahne, W. (1973) Isolation and characterization of agent causing swim bladder infl ammation in carp. Nature 244, 235–237.

25. Bachmann, P.A. and Ahne, W. (1974) Biological properties and identifi cation of the agent causing swim bladder infl ammation in carp. Archiv für Gesamte Virusforschung 44, 261–269.

26. Bagum, N., Monir, M. S., & Khan, M. H. (2013). Present status of fish diseases and economic losses due to incidence of disease in rural freshwater aquaculture of Bangladesh. Journal of Innov. Dev. Strategy, 7(3), 48-53.

27. Bassey, S.E., A Concise Dictionary of Parasitology. 1st Edn., Zetus Concepts, Port Harcourt, pp: 115, 2011

28. Bataillon E., Moeller A., and Terre L, (1902), tuber die Identitit des Bacillus des Karpfens (Bataillon, Dubard, and Terre) und des Bacillus der Blindschleiche (Moeller) Z. Tuberk., 3, 467-469.

29. Bataillon, E., and Terre, L., (1897). La form saprophytique de la tuberculose humaine et de la tuberculose aviare. Comp. rend., 124, 1399-1400.

30. Baudouy, A.M. (1975) Virémie printanière de la carpe: premiers isolements du virus en France. Bulletin de l'Office International des Épizooties 83, 717–722.

31. Bekesi, L. and Szabo, E. (1979) A rhabdovirus isolated from carps in Hungary. Experimental infection of carps and resistance of the virus. Acta Microbiologica Academiae Scientiarum Hungaricae 26, 193–197.

32. Bernardet, J.F., Campbell, A.C. and Buswell, J.A., (1990). Flexibacter maritimus is the agent of 'black patch necrosis' in Dover sole in Scotland. Dis. Aquat. Org., 8: 233-237

33. Bertolini, J.M. and Rohovec, J.S. (1992). Electrophoretic detection of proteases from different Flavobacterium columnare strains and assessment of their variability. Dis. Aquat. Org., 12: 121-128.

34. Bhattacharya, U. (1995) Sensitivity test of certain antimicrobial agents on AspergiUus terreus Thorn. fish fnngal isolates of Channa punctatus in vitro. Environ Ecol 13:976-978,

35. Bhowmik P, Bag P.K, Hajra T.K., De R, Sarkar P, Ramamurthy T. (2009) Pathogenic potential of Aeromonas hydrophila isolated from surface waters in Kolkata, India. J Med. Microbiol.; 58:1549-1558.

36. Bly J. E., Lawson LA, Szalai AJ, (1993). Environmental factors affecting outbreaks of winter Saprolegniosis in channel catfish, Ictaluruspunctatus (Rafinesque).J Fish Dis 16:541- 549,

37. Bondad-Reantaso, M.G., Subasinghe, R.P., Arthur, J.R., et al. (2005) Disease and health management in Asian aquaculture. Veterinary Parasitology, 132, 249–272.

38. Bootsma, R. and Ebregt, D. Spring viremia of carp. In: Anderson, D.P., Dorson, M. and Dubourget, P. (eds) Antigens of Fish Pathogens. Collection Fondation Marcel Mérieux, Lyons, France, pp. 81–86. 1983

39. Bootsma, R., Fijan, N. and Blommaert, J. (1977) Isolation and preliminary identifi cation of the causative agent of carp erthrodermatitis. Veterinarski Arhiv 47, 291–302.

40. Brudeseth B.E., Castric J. & Evensen O. (2002) Studies on pathogenesis following single and double infection with viral hemorrhagic septicemia virus and infectious hematopoietic necrosis virus in rainbow trout (Oncorhynchus mykiss). Veterinary Pathology 39, 180–189.

41. Bruno, D. W., & Stamps, D. J. (1987). Saprolegniasis of Atlantic salmon, Salmo salar L., fry. Journal of Fish Diseases, 10(6), 513-517.

42. Bucke, D. and Finlay, J. (1979) Identifi cation of spring viraemia in carp (Cyprinus carpio L.) in Great Britain. Veterinary Record 104, 69–71.

43. Buller, Nicky B. Bacteria from fish and other aquatic animals: a practical identification manual. Cabi, 2004.

44. Ch. Sarojnalini and Abdul Hei (2019). Fish as an Important Functional Food for Quality Life, Functional Foods, Vasiliki Lagouri, IntechOpen, DOI: 10.5772/intechopen.81947.

45. Chen, M.F., Henry-Ford, D. and Groff, J.M., (1995). Isolation and characterization of Flexibacter maritimus from marine fishes of California. J. Aquat. Anim. Health, 7: 318- 326.

46. Cipriano, R.C., Bullock G.L., Pyle S.W. Aeromonas hydrophila and Motile Aeromonad Septicemias of Fish. Fish Disease Leaflet 68, US

Department of the Interior Fish & Wildlife Service, Washington. 2001

47. Clayton, G.M. and Price D.J. (1992). Interspecific and intraspecific variation in resistance to ichthyophthiriasis among poeciliid and goodeid fishes. Journal of Fish Biology 40, 445- 453.

48. Cotruvo J. A., Dufour A., Rees G., Bartram J., Carr R., Cliver D.O. Waterborne Zoonoses: Identification, Causes and Control. World Health Organization, IWA Publishing, London, U.K. 2004

49. Crow GL, Brock JA, Kaiser S (1995). Fusarium solani fnngal infection of the lateral line canal system in captive scalloped hammerhead sharks (Sphyra lewini) in Hawaii.J Wildl Dis 31:562-565,

50. Cusack, R. and D.K. Cone, (1986). A review of parasites as vectors of viral and bacterial diseases of fishes. J. Fish Dis., 9: 169-171.

51. Das, A., Sahoo, P. K., Mohanty, B. R., & Jena, J. K. (2011). Pathophysiology of experimental Aeromonas hydrophila infection in Puntius sarana: early changes in blood and aspects of the innate immune-related gene expression in survivors. Veterinary immunology and immunopathology, 142(3-4), 207-218.

52. Dey, R. K. (1989). Histopathology of Argulosis in the Indian Major carp, Labeo rohita (Hamilton), Proc. Natl. Sem. On 'Forty Years of Aquaculture 'in India: 7-9 Nov., 1989, pp. SVP/6.

53. Dikkeboom, A.L., Radi, C., Toohey-Kurth, K., Marcquenski, S.V., Engel, M. et al. (2004) First report of spring viremia of carp virus (SVCV) in wild common carp in North America. Journal of Aquatic Animal Health 16, 169–178.

54. Dixon, P.F. (1997) Immunization with viral antigens: viral diseases of carp and catfish. In: Gudding, R., Lillehaug, A., Midtlyng, P.J. and Brown, F. (eds) Fish Vaccinology. Karger, Basel, pp. 221–232.

55. Dixon, P.F. (2008) Virus diseases of cyprinids. In: Eiras, J.C., Segner, H., Wahli, T. and Kapoor, B.G. (eds) Fish Diseases. Science Publishers, Enfield, New Hampshire, pp. 87–184.

56. Dixon, P.F., Hattenberger-Baudouy, A.M. and Way, K. (1994) Detection of carp antibodies to spring viraemia of carp virus by a competitive immunoassay. Diseases of Aquatic Organisms 19, 181–186.

57. Dixon, P.F., Smail, D.A., Algoet, M., Hastings, T.S., Bayley, A. et al. (2012) Studies on the effect

of temperature and pH on the inactivation of fish viral and bacterial pathogens. Journal of Fish Diseases 35, 51–64.

58. Doty M.S, Slater D.W. (1946). A new species of Heterosporium pathogen on young chinook salmon. Am Midl Nat 36:663-665,

59. Dudgeon D., Arthington A.H., Gessner M.O., Kawabata Z., Knowler D.J., Leveque C. et al. (2006) Freshwater biodiversity: importance, threats, status and conservation challenges. Biological Reviews, 81, 163–182.

60. Ebert, D. (1998) Experimental evolution of parasites. Science 282, 1432–1435. (doi:10.1126/science.282.5393.1432)

61. Edwards, R.H. and R.M. Overstreet, (1976). Mesenchymal tumors of some estuarine fishes of the northern gulf of Mexico. I. Subcutaneous tumors, probably fibrosarcomas, in the striped mullet, Mugil cephalus. Bull. Mar. Sci., 26: 33-40.

62. Egusa S. Fungal Diseases, in Kothekar KS (ed) : Infectious Diseases of Fish. New Delhi, India, Oxoian Press Pvt Ltd, 1991, pp 368-421

63. Ellis A.E., Waddell I.F., Minter D.W. (1983) A systemic fungal disease in Atlantic salmon parr,

Salmo salarL, caused by a species of Phialiophora.J Fish Dis 6:511-523.

64. Elsayed, E., Faisal, M., Thomas, M., Whelan, G., Batts, W., Winton, J., (2006). Isolation of viral haemorrhagic septicaemia virus from muskellunge, Esox masquinongy (Mitchill), in Lake St Clair, Michigan, USA reveals a new sublineage of the North American genotype. J. Fish Dis. 29, 611–619.

65. Faisal, M. and Ahne, W. (1984) Spring viremia of carp virus (SVCV): comparison of immunoperoxidase, fl uorescent antibody and cell culture isolation techniques for detection of antigen. Journal of Fish Diseases 7, 57–64.

66. FAO (2007) State of the World Aquaculture 2006. FAO Fisheries Technical Paper No. 500. FAO, Rome, 134 pp

67. FAO, Te State of World Fisheries and Aquaculture, Contributing to food security and nutrition for all, Food and Agriculture Organization of the United Nations, Rome, Italy, 2016.

68. Federal Joint Subcommittee on Aquaculture: Guide to drug, vaccine and pesticide use in aquaculture, Texas Agriculture Extension Service, Texas A&M University, College Station, Texas, 1994

69. Fijan, N. Infectious dropsy in carp – a disease complex. In: Mawdesley-Thomos, L.E. (ed.) Diseases of Fish. Symposia of the Zoological Society of London. Academic Press, London, pp. 39– 51. 1972

70. Fijan, N. Spring viremia of carp (SVC) A review. In: Dill, W.A. (ed.) Symposium on the Major Communicable Fish Diseases in Europe and Their Control. EIFAC (European Inland Fisheries Advisory Commission) Technical Paper 17, Supplement 2, Rome, pp. 119–123,1973.

71. Fijan, N. Advances in knowledge of viral diseases of fi sh. In: Page, L.A. (ed.) Wildlife Diseases. Plenum Press, New York, pp. 127–133, 1975.

72. Fijan, N. Vaccination of fish in European pond culture: prospects and constraints. In: Oláh, J. (ed.) Fish, Pathogens and Environment in European Polyculture. Akademiai Kiado, Budapest, pp. 233–241,1984.

73. Fijan, N. () Vaccination against spring viraemia of carp. In: Ellis, A.E. (ed.) Fish Vaccination. Academic Press, London, pp. 204–215,1988.

74. Fijan, N. Spring viraemia of carp and other viral diseases and agents of warm-water fish. In: Woo, P.T.K. and Bruno, D.W. (eds) Fish Diseases and Disorders, Volume 3: Viral, Bacterial and Fungal

Infections, 1st edn. CAB International, Wallingford, UK, pp. 177–244,1999.

75. Fijan, N., Petrinec, Z., Sulimanovic , D. and Zwillenberg, L.O. (1971) Isolation of the viral causative agent from the acute form of infectious dropsy of carp. Veterinarski Arhiv 41, 125–138.

76. Folke, C., Carpenter, S., Walker, B., Scheffer, M., Elmqvist, T., Gunderson, L., Holling, C. S., (2004). Regime shifts, resilience, and biodiversity in ecosystem management. Annu. Rev. Ecol. Evol. Syst. 35, 557–581.

77. Francis-Floyd R, Noga E.J. Medical management of channel catfish. Part I. Types of skin and gill pathogens. Compend Contin Educ Pract Vet 16:808-814, 1994

78. Gaafar, A.Y., Vesely, T., Nakai, T., El-Manakhly, E.M., Soliman, M.K. et al. (2011) Histopathological and ultrastructural study of experimental spring viraemia of carp (SVC) infection of common carp with comparison between different immunohistodignostic techniques efficacy. Life Science Journal 8, 523–533.

79. Getchell, R. G., Culligan, W. J., Kirchgessner, M., Sutton, C. A., Casey, R. M., Bowser, P. R., (2006). Quantitative polymerase chain reaction assay used to measure the prevalence of

Clostridium botulinum type E in fish in the lower Great Lakes. J. Aquat. Anim Health 18, 39–50.

80. Gonzalez, M.P., Sanchez, X., Ganga, M.A., Lopez-Lastra, M., Jashes, M. and Sandino, A.M.(1997). Detection of the infectious hematopoietic necrosis virus directly from infected fish tissues by dot blot hybridisation with a non-radioactive probe. J. Virol. Methods, 65: 273–279.

81. Goodwin, A.E. (2003) Differential diagnosis: SVCV vs KHV in koi. Fish Health Newsletter, American Fisheries Society, Fish Health Section 31, 9–13.

82. Gopalakrishnan (1961). Observations on infectious dropsy of Indian major carps and its experimental induction. J. Scient. Indl. Res, 20: 357-58.

83. Gopalakrishnan V, Gupta PD. (1960) An eye disease which causes mortality of the Catla catla (Hamilton Buch.) Curr Sci; 29(6):240.

84. Gopalakrishnan V., (1963). Controlling pest and diseases of cultured fishes, Indian livestock;1(1):51-54.

85. Grabowshi L.D., La Patra S.E., Cain K.D. (2004). Systemic and mucosal antibody response in tilapia, Oreochromis niloticus (L.), following

immunization with Flavobacterium columnare. J Fish Dis; 27:573-581.

86. Haenen, O.L.M. and Hedrick, R.P. (2006) Koi herpesvirus workshop. Bulletin of the European Association of Fish Pathologists 26, 26–37.

87. Harvell C.D., Kim K., Burkholder J.M., Colwell R.R., Epstein P.R., Grimes D.J. et al. (1999) Review: marine ecology – emerging marine diseases – climate links and anthropogenic factors. Science, 285, 1505–1510.

88. Harvell C.D., Mitchell C.E., Ward J.R., Altizer S.A., Dobson A.P., Ostfeld R.S., et al. (2002) Climate warming and disease risks for terrestrial and marine biota. Science, 296, 2158–2162.

89. Håstein, T., Binde, M., Hine, M., Johnsen, S., Lillehaug, A. et al. (2008) National biosecurity approaches, plans and programmes in response to diseases in farmed aquatic animals: evolution, effectiveness and the way forward. Revue Scientifique et Technique 27, 125–145.

90. Hatai K, Egusa S: Candida sake from gastrotympanitis of Amago, Oncorhynchus rodurus. Bull Jap Soc Sci Fish 41:993, 1975.

91. Hatai K, FujimakiY, Egusa S: Avisceral mycosis in ayu fry, Plecoglossus altivelis Temminck &

Schlegel, caused by a species of Phoma.J Fish Dis 9:111-116, 1986

92. Hawkins, W.E., R.M. Overstreet and W.W. Walker, (1988). Small fish models for identifying carcinogens in the aqueous environment. Water Res. Bull., 24: 941-949.

93. Hedrick, R. P., (1998). Relationships of the host, pathogen, and environment: implications for diseases of cultured and wild fish populations. J. Aquat. Anim. Health 10, 107–111.

94. Hill B. (1992) Impact of viral diseases on salmonid fish in Europe. In: Proceedings of the OJI International Symposium on Salmonid Diseases (ed. by T. Kimura), Hokkaido University Press, Sapporo, Japan.

95. Hill, B.J. (1977) Studies on SVC virulence and immunization. Bulletin de l'Offi ce International des Épizooties 87, 455–456.

96. Hines RS, Wohlfarth GW, Moav R. & Hulata. G., (1974). Genetic differences in susceptibility to two disease among strains of the common carp. Aquaculture 3, 187-197.

97. Hoffmann, B., Beer, M., Schütze, H. and Mettenleiter, T.C. (2005). Fish rhabdoviruses: molecular epidemiology and evolution. Current

Topics in Microbiology and Immunology 292, 81-117.

98. Holey,M. E., Elliott, R. F.,Marcquenski, S. V., Hnath, J. G., Smith, K. D., (1998). Chinook salmon epizootics in Lake Michigan: possible contributing factors and management implications. J. Aquat. Anim. Health 10, 202–210.

99. Hora, S. L. and Pillay, T. V. R. (1962). Handbook on fish culture in the Indo- Pacific region, FAO Fish, Biol. Techn. Paper (14) : 204.

100. Huizinga HW, Esch GW, Hazen TC. (1979) Histopathology of red-sore disease (Aeromonas hydrophila) in naturally and experimentally infected largemouth bass Micropterus salmoides (Lacepede). J Fish Dis.; 2:263-277.

101. Hussain SM, M Javed, A Javid, T Javid and N Hussain, (2011). Growth responses of Catla catla, Labeo rohita and Cirrhina mrigala during chronic exposure of iron. Pak J Agric Sci, 48: 225-230.

102. J. Kubecka, D. S. Boukal, M. Cech (2016), "Ecology and ecological ˇ quality of fsh in lakes and reservoirs," Fisheries Research, vol. 173, pp. 1–3,.

103. J. Romero, C. G. Feijoo, and P. Navarrete, "Antibiotics in aquaculture Use, abuse and alternatives," Health and Environment in Aquaculture, pp. 160–198, 2012.

104. Jeremic, S., Dobrila, J.D. and Radosavljevic, V. (2004) Dissemination of spring viraemia of carp (SVC) in Serbia during the period 1992–2002. Acta Veterinaria (Beograd) 54, 289–299.

105. Jhingran,V.G.(1991). Textbook of fish and fisheries of India, Third edition, HindustanPublishing corporation (India), Delhi, 1991.

106. Karunasagar, I., P. K. M . Manzoor Ali; G. Jeyasekaran and I. Karunasagar (1986). Ulcerative form of Aeromonas hydrophila infection of Catla catla.Current Science. Dec.5, Vol. 55, No. 23, pp., 194-95.

107. Khoo L, Leard AT, Waterstrat PR, et al: Branchiomyces infection in farm-reared channel catfish, Ictaluruspunctatus (Rafinesque).J Fish Dis 21:423-431, 1998

108. Kirpichnikov, V.S., Ilyasov, J.I., Shart, L.A., Vikhman, A.A., Ganchenko, M.V. et al. (1993) Selection of Krasnodar common carp (Cyprinus carpio L.) for resistance to dropsy: principal results and prospects. Aquaculture 111, 7–20.

109. Kiryu, I., Sakai, T., Kurita, J. and Iida, T. (2007) Virucidal effect of disinfectants on spring viremia of carp virus. Fish Pathology 42, 111–113.

110. Kitancharoen N, Hatai K, Yamamoto A (1997) Aquatic fungi developing on eggs of salmonids. J Aquat Anim Health 9:314-316,

111. Klinger RE, Floyd RF. Fungal diseases of fish. Fact sheet VM 97, FAIRS, Florida; 1996.

112. Kölbl, O. (1980). Dianostic de la viremia printaniere de la carpe et essais d'immunisation contre cette maladie. Bulletin de I'Office Intern

113. Kölbl, O. and Kainz, E. (1977) Die V erbreitung des Erregers der infektiösen Bauchwassersucht bzw. der Frühlingsvirämie in den österreichischen Karpfenteichwirtschaften. Österreichs Fischerei 30, 80–83.

114. Kumar , D, (1989). Epizootic ulcerative syndrome outbreak in India. Summer Inst. On Fish Dis. Dia & health Man. In Freshwat. Aqua. Syst., 5-24 June, CIFA

115. Kumar D., Mishra B.K. and Dey R.K. (1986 a). Dropsy of Catla catla (Ham) caused by amixed infection of Aeromonas hydrophila and Myxosporidian sp., Aquaculture Hungarica (Szarvas), V : 107-112.

116. Kumar, D., R. K . Dey, B. K. Mishra and K. Kumar (1987 a). Ulcerative disease in Catla catla (Ham).Research Highlights in the First Indian Fisheries Forum, Dec.6- 10, Mangalore,India.

117. Kumar, D., R. K. Dey and K. Kumar (1986 d). Preliminary observations of gill hyperplasia in common carp, Cyprinus carpio (L), Abst. In the proc,. of 'International Symp. On Ichthyology', held in Dubronik, Yugoslavia, Sept., 1986.

118. Kumaraiah, P. V. K. Murgesan and P. V. Dehadrai (1971). A new record of a bacterium causing eye disease and mortality in Channa maruatius (Ham), J. Inland, Fish. Soc. India, 9:214-15.

119. Kunttu, H. M. T., Valtonen, E. T., Jokinen, E. I. & Suomalainen, R. (2009). Saprophytism of a fish pathogen as a transmission strategy. Epidemiology 1, 96–100. (doi:10.1016/j.epidem.2009.04.003).

120. Kuzmin, I.V., Novella, I.S., Dietzgen, R.G., Padhi, A. and Rupprecht, C.E. (2009) The rhabdoviruses: biodiversity, phylogenetics, and evolution. Infection, Genetics and Evolution 9, 541– 553.

121. Lafferty K.D., Porter J.W. & Ford S.E. (2004) Are diseases increasing in the ocean?

Annual Reviews of Ecology Evolution and Systematics, 35, 31–54.

122. Langdon JS, MacDonald WL (1987) Cranial Exophilia piscphilia infection in Salmo salar in Australia. Bull Eur Assoc Fish Pathol 7:35-37,

123. Lightner D, Redman RM, Mohney L (1988) A renal mycosis of an adult hybrid red tilapia Oreochromis mossambicus X O. hornorum, caused by the imperfect fungus, Paecilomyces marquandii. J Fish Dis 11:437-440,

124. Lilley J.H, Inglis V (1997) Comparative effects of various antibiotics, fungicides and disinfectants on Aphanomyces invaders and other saprolegniaceous fungi. Aquacult Res 28:461-469.

125. Lipton, A P (2006), Diseases of Ornamental Fishes and their control, Central Marine Fisheries Research Institute,109.

126. Madhuri S, Mandloi, AK, Pandey Govind, Srivastav AB., (2012). Transgenic fishmodel in environmental toxicology, Int Res J Pharm, 3(5):37-40).

127. McCallum H.I., Kuris A., Harvell C.D., Lafferty K.D., Smith G.W. & Porter J. (2004) Does terrestrial epidemiology apply to marine

systems? Trends in Ecology and Evolution, 19, 585–591.

128. McGinnis MR, Ajello L: A new species of Exophilia isolated from channel catfish. Mycologia 66:518-520, 1974

129. McKeand, J.B (1998).Molecular diagnosis of parasitic nematodes. Parasitology, 117: 87– 96.

130. McNinch R.M., Rose J.B. & Dreelin E.A. (2009) Aquatic ecosystems and human health. In: Encyclopedia of Inland Waters (Ed. G.E. Likens), pp. 13–20. Elsevier, Oxford, U.K.

131. Meng HL, Wise DJ, Robinson EH: Chemical prevention and treatment of winter Saprolegniosis ("winter kill") in channel catfish Ictalurus punctatus. J World Aquacult Soc 27(1):1-6, 1996

132. Meyer FP, Robinson JA (1973). Branchiomycosis: A new fungal disease of North American Fishes. Prog Fish-Cult 35:74- 77.

133. Mishra, S. S., Rakesh, D., Dhiman, M., Choudhary, P., Debbarma, J., Sahoo, S. N., & Mishra, C. K. (2017). Present status of fish disease management in freshwater aquaculture in India: state-of-the-art-review. Journal of Aquaculture & Fisheries, 1(003).

134. Misk, E., Garver, K.A., Nagy, E., Isaacs, S., Tubbs, L. et al. (2016) Pathogenesis of spring viremia of carp virus in emerald shiner Notropis atherinoides Rafinesque, fathead minnow Pimephales promelas Rafinesque and white sucker Catostomus commersonii (Lacepede). Journal of Fish Diseases 39, 729–739.

135. Mitchell, A. J., 2001. Finfish health in the United States (1609 – 1969): historical perspective, pioneering researchers and fish health workers, and annotated bibliography. Aquaculture 196, 347–438.

136. Miyazaki T, Kubota S, Tashiro F (1977) Studies on visceral mycosis of salmonid fry--I. Histopathology. Fish Pathol 11:183-186.

137. Moffitt, C. M., Stewart, B. C, LaPatra, S. E., Brunson, R. D., Bartholomew, J. L., Peterson, J. E., Amos, K. H., (1998). Pathogens and diseases of fish in aquatic ecosystems: implications in fisheries management. J. Aquat. Anim. Health 10, 95–100.

138. Mohan, C. V., & Bhatta, R. (2002). Social and economic impacts of aquatic animal health problems on aquaculture in India. FAO Fisheries Technical Paper, 63-75.

139. Mohanty, B. R., & Sahoo, P. K. (2007). Edwardsiellosis in fish: a brief review. Journal of biosciences, 32(3), 1331-1344.

140. Molnár, K. and Csaba, G. (2005) Sanitary management in Hungarian aquaculture. Veterinary Research Communications 29, 143–146.

141. Mukherjee, S. C. (2002). Fish diseases in India, their causes and control measures-Winter school on recent advances in diagnosis and management of diseases in mariculture, 7th to 27th November 2002, Course Manual.

142. Mukherjee, S. C., Suresh Chandra and Kausalya Nayak (1991). Studies on biochemical differences among isolates of Aeromonas hydrophila obtained from ulcerative disease affected fishes.Proc. Nat. Symp.On New Horizons in Fresh.

143. Musa N, Wei LS, Shaharom F, Wee W. (2008) Surveillance of Bacteria Species in Diseased Freshwater Ornamental Fish from Aquarium Shop. World Applied Sciences Journal.; 3:903-905.

144. Nayak and S. C. Mukherjee (1994). Drug resistance of Aeromonas hydrophila strains isolated from freshwater and brackishwater fises. Fishing Chimes, Sept., 1994: 41-42.

145. Neish GA, Hughes GC: Fungal Diseases of Fishes. Neptune, NJ, TFH Publications, 1980.

146. Nepszy, S. J., Budd, J., Dechtiar, A. O., 1978. Mortality of young of the year rainbow smelt (Osmerus mordax) in Lake Erie associated with the occurrence of Glugea hertwigi. J. Wildl. Diseases 14, 233–239.

147. Noga EJ (1993) Water mold infectious of freshwater fishes: Recent advances. Ann Rev Fish Dis 3:291-304,

148. Oidtmann, B.C., Thrush, M.A., Denham, K.L. and Peeler, E.J. (2011) International and national biosecurity strategies in aquatic animal health. Aquaculture 320, 22–33.

149. OIE (2006) Manual of Diagnostic Tests for Aquatic Animals, 6th edn. World Organisation for Animal Health, Paris, 469 pp.

150. OIE (2009a) Aquatic Animal Health Code, 12th edn. World Organisation for Animal Health, Paris, 265 pp.

151. OIE (2015a) Spring viraemia of carp. In: Manual of Diagnostic Tests for Aquatic Animals. World Organisation for Animal Health, Paris. Updated 2016 version (Chapter 2.3.9.) available at: http://www.oie.

int/index.php?id=2439&L=0&htmfile=chapitre_svc. htm (accessed 31 October 2016).

152. Olesen N.J. (1998) Sanitation of viral haemorrhagic septicaemia (VHS). Journal of Applied Ichthyology 14, 173–177.

153. Olivares-Fuster, O., Baker, J. L., Terhune, J. S., Shoemaker, C. A., Klesius, P. H. & Arias, C. R. 2007 Host-specific association between Flavobacterium columnare genomovars and fish species. Syst. Appl. Microbiol. 30, 624 –633. (doi:10.1016/j.syapm.2007.07.003).

154. Olufemi BE, Agius C, Roberts RJ (1983). Aspergillomycosis in intensively cultured tilapia from Kenya. Vet Rec 112:203- 204.

155. Oraic, D. and Zrncic, S. (2005) An overview of health control in Croatian aquaculture. Veterinary Research Communications 29, 139–142.

156. Osadcaja, E.F. (1964) Vydelenie citopatogennyh agentov ot karpov pri ostroi formi krasnukhi. Veterinarija 41, 29 [in Russian].

157. Osadchaya, E.F. and Rudenko, A.P. (1981) Patogennost virusov, vydelennyh pri krasnuhe (vesennej viremii) karpov i kliniko-morfologicheskaja harakteristika estestvennogo techenija bolezni i v eksperimente [Pathogenicity

of viruses isolated from carp with infectious dropsy (red-spot disease, spring viraemia) and clinical and morphological characteristics of the course of the natural and experimental disease]. Rybnoe Khozyaistvo (Kiev) 32, 66–71.

158. Ostfeld R.S., Keesing F. & Eviner V.T. (2008). Infectious Disease Ecology: Effects of Ecosystems on Disease and of Disease on Ecosystems. Princeton University Press, Princeton, NJ.

159. Otte E: Eine mykose bei einem Stachelrochen (Trigon pastinacae L.). Weiner Tierarztl Monatschr 51:171-175, 1964

160. Pal , R. N. and S. D. Tripathi (1970). Use of terramycin for fish diseases in carp and catfish culture in Indian waters. J. Inland Fish. Soc., 10: 166-68.

161. Pal RN, Ghose AK. An effective method of controlling tail and fin rot in Indian major carps. J Inland Fish Soc 1975; 7: 98-99.

162. Pandey Govind, Madhuri S, Mandloi AK. Immunostimulant effect of medicinal plants on fish. Int Res J Pharm 2012; 3(3):112-114.

163. Paperna, I., (1973). Lymphocystis in fish from East African Lakes. J. Wild. Dis., 9: 331-335.

164. Parveen, R., Ahmed, G. U., & Ali, M. L. (2005). Seasonal variation of diseases of some small indigenous fishes from Oxbow Lake fisheries of Bangladesh. Pakistan Journal of Zoology, 37(1), 53-59.

165. Pazos, F., Santos, Y., Macías, A.R., Núñez, S. and Toranzo, A.E. (1996). Evaluation of media for the successful culture of Flexibacter maritimus. J. Fish Dis., 19: 193-197

166. Peeler E. J. and Taylor, N. G., (2011) "Te application of epidemiology in aquatic animal health - opportunities and challenges," Veterinary Research, 42 (1), 94-99

167. Phelps, N.B.D., Armien, A.G., Mor, S.K., Goyal, S.M., Warg, J.V. et al. (2012) Spring viremia of carp virus in Minnehaha Creek, Minnesota. Journal of Aquatic Animal Health 24, 232–237.

168. Pierotti P (1971) Su di un particolare episodio di micosi in Tinca tinca. Atti Soc Ital Sci Vet 25:361-363,

169. Post G: Textbook of Fish Health. Neptune City, NJ, TFH Publications, 1987

170. Prichard, R. (1997). Application of molecular biology in veterinary parasitology. Vet.

171. Pyle, S.W. and Shotts, E.B. (1980). A new approach for differentiating flexibacteria isolated from cold water and warm water fish. Can. J. Fish. Aquat. Sci., 37: 1040-1042.

172. Quiniou SMA, Bigler S, Clem LW, (1998). Effects of water temperature on mucous cell distribution in channel catfish epidermis: a factor in winter saprolegniasis. Fish Shellf Immunol 8:1-11,

173. R. Gudding, "Vaccination as a Preventive Measure," in Fish Vaccination, R. Gudding, A. Lillehaug, and O. Evensen, Eds., vol. 1st, pp. 12–21, John Wiley & Sons, Inc, Oxford, UK, 2014.

174. R. Harikrishnan, C. Balasundaram, and M.S. Heo, (2011). "Fish health aspects in grouper aquaculture," Aquaculture, vol. 320, no. 1-2, pp. 1–21.

175. Ragan MA, Goggin CL, Cawthorn RJ, (1996). A novel clade of protistan parasites near the animal fungal divergence. Proc Natl Acad Sci USA 93:11907-11912,

176. Rand, T. G., & Munden, D. (1992). Enzyme involvement in the invasion of brook char, Salvelinus fontinalis (Mitchill), eggs by Saprolegnia diclina (Oomycotina:

Saprolegniaceae). Journal of Fish Diseases, 15(1), 91-94.

177. Rapport, D. J., Constanza, R., McMichael, A. J., 1998. Assessing ecosystem health. Trends Eco. Evol. 13, 397–402. Rapport, D. J., 1999. Epidemiology and Ecosystem Hea.

178. Rehulka, J. (1996) Blood parameters in common carp with spontaneous spring viremia (SVC). Aquaculture International 4, 175–182.

179. Roberts RJ. Motile aeromonad septicaemia. In Bacteriology of Fish Disease. Eds V. Inglis, R. Roberts, N. Bromage. Blackwell Scientific Publications, 1993, 143-155. 21.

180. Roberts RJ: The mycology of teleosts, in Roberts RJ (ed): Fish Pathology, 2nd edition. London, England, Baillere Tindall, 1989, pp 320-336

181. Roberts, L., Janovy, R., & Schimidt, G. (2005). Foundations of Parasitology. New York, NY: McGraw Hill Publishers.

182. Rodak, L., Pospisil, Z., Tomanek, J., Vesely, T., Obr, T. and Valicek, L. (1993) Enzyme-linked immunosorbent assay (ELISA) for the detection of spring viraemia of carp virus (SVCV) in tissue homogenates of the carp. Journal of Fish Diseases 16, 108–111.

183. Ross AJ, Yasutake WT (1973). Scolecobasidum humicola, a fungal pathogen of fish. J Fish Res Board Can 30:994-995.

184. Rubbani B, M Afzal, MS Mubarik, M Salim and SM Hussain, (2011). Estimation of apparent digestibility coefficients of soybean meal based diets with different protein levels for Labeo rohita. Pak J Agric Sci, 48: 231-235

185. Rudikov, N.I., Grišecenko, L.I. and Lobuncov, K.A. (1975) Vesennaja virusnaja boleznj ryb. Bjulletin Vsesojuznogo Ordeni Lenina Institut Eksperimentaljnoj Veterinarii, Moskva 20, 16–19 [in Russian]

186. Sahoo, P. K., Mohanty, J., Garnayak, S. K., Mohanty, B. R., Kar, B., Prasanth, H., & Jena, J. K. (2013). Estimation of loss due to argulosis in carp culture ponds in India. Indian J Fish, 60(2), 99-102.

187. Sandeep. P, C. D. . and K. P. . (2016). Present status of Parasitic and Bacterial diseases in Fresh Water Fish Seed Farms in East Godavari District, Andhra Pradesh P.Sandeep 1 *, B.Chamundeswari Devi 2 and K.Phaneendra Kumar 3 1. 117–122.

188. Sanil, N. K., Suja, G., Lijo, J., & Vijayan, K. K. (2012). First report of Perkinsus beihaiensis in Crassostrea madrasensis from the Indian subcontinent. Diseases of Aquatic Organisms, 98(3), 209-220.

189. Sano, M., Nakai, K. and Fijan, N. (2011) Viral diseases and agents of warmwater fish. In: Woo, P.T.K. and Bruno, D.W. (eds) Fish Diseases and Disorders, Volume 3: Viral, Bacterial and Fungal Infections, 2nd edn. CAB International, Wallingford, UK, pp. 166– 244.

190. Schaumann K, Priebe I- Onchroconis humicola causing muscular black spot disease of Atlantic salmon (Salmo salar). CanJ Bot 72:1629-1634, 1994

191. Sen, K., & Mandal, R. (2018). Fresh-water fish diseases in west Bengal, India. Internafional Journal of Fisheries and Aquafic Studies, 6, 356-362.

192. Sha J, Koslova E, Chopra A. (2002) Role of various enterotoxins in Aeromonas hydrophila-induced gastroenteritis: generation of enterotoxin gene-deficient mutants and evaluation of their enterotoxic activity. Infection and Immunity.; 70:1924-193 22.

193. Shaoqi, L. (1989). Main fish diseases and their control.

194. Shome R, Shome BR. (1999) A typical chronic form of Aeromonas hydrophila infection in Indian major carp, Catla catla, from Andaman. Curr. Sci.; 76:1188- 1190.

195. Skall H.F., Slierendrecht W.J., King J.A. & Olesen N.J. (2004) Experimental infection of rainbow trout Oncorhynchus mykiss with viral haemorrhagic septicaemia virus isolates from European marine and farmed fishes. Diseases of Aquatic Organisms 58, 99–110.

196. Sniezko, S. (1974) The effect of environmental stress on outbreaks of infectious diseases of fishes. J. Fish Biol. 6, 197 –208.

197. Spanggaard B, Skouboe PO, Rossen L: Phylogenetic relationships of the intercellular fish pathogen Ichthyophonus hoferi and fungi, choano-flagellates and the rosette agent. Mar Biol126:1109-1115, 1996.

198. Srivasta RC: Fish Mycopathology. New Delhi, India, Today & Tomorrow's Printers and Publishers, 1987

199. Stone, D.M., Ahne, W., Denham, K.D., Dixon, P.F., Liu, C.T.Y. et al. (2003) Nucleotide sequence analysis of the glycoprotein gene of putative spring viraemia of carp virus and pike fry rhabdovirus isolates reveals four genogroups. Diseases of Aquatic Organisms 53, 203–210.

200. Strongman DB, Morrison CM, McClelland G: Lesions in the musculature of captive American plaice Hippoglossoides platessoides caused by the fungus Hormoconis resinae (Deuteromycetes). Dis Aquat Org 28:107-113, 1997

201. Subasinghe, R. P. (2005). Epidemiological approach to aquatic animal health management: opportunities and challenges for developing countries to increase aquatic production through aquaculture. Preventive veterinary medicine, 67(2-3), 117-124.

202. Sulimanovic, M. (1973) Immunity of carp to Rhabdovirus carpio and determination of antibodies by indirect haemagglutination. Veterinarski Arhiv 43, 153–161.

203. Swaminathan, T. R., Kumar, R., Dharmaratnam, A., Basheer, V. S., Sood, N., Pradhan, P. K., ... & Jena, J. K. (2016). Emergence of carp edema virus in cultured ornamental koi carp, Cyprinus carpio koi, in India. Journal of General Virology, 97(12), 3392-3399.

204. Taylor, N.G.H., Peeler, E.J., Denham, K.L., Crane, C.N., Thrush, M.A. et al. (2013) Spring viraemia of carp (SVC) in the UK: the road to freedom. Preventive Veterinary Medicine 111, 156–164.

205. Tesarcík, J., Macura, B., Dedek, L., Valícek, D. and Smíd, B. (1977) Isolation and electron microscopy of rhabdovirus from the acute form of infectious dropsy of carp (spring viremia of carp). Zentralblatt für Veterinärmedizin (B) 24, 340–343.

206. Thompson KD, Lilley JH, Chen S-C, (1999). The immune response of rainbow trout (Oncorhynchus mykiss) against Aphanomyces invadans. Fish Shellf Immunol 9:195-210,

207. Tomašec, I., Brudnjak, Z., Fijan, N. and Kunst, L. (1964) Weiterer Beitrag zur Atiologie der Infektioser Bauchwassersucht des Karpfens. Bulletin International, Jugoslavenska Akademija Znanosti i Umjetnosti Zagreb 16, 191–193.

208. Tucker CS, Robinson EH: Channel Catfish Farming Handbook. New York, Van Nostrand Reinhold, 1990, pp 317-380

209. Kumar. V., S. Roy, D. K. Meena, and U. K. Sarkar, "Application of probiotics in shrimp aquaculture: importance, mechanisms of action, and methods of administration," Reviews in Fisheries Science and Aquaculture, vol. 24, no. 4, pp. 342–368, 2016.

210. Van Oosten, J., (1944). Mortality of smelt, Osmerus mordax (Mitchill), in lakes Huron and Michigan during the fall and winter of 1942–1943. Trans. Am. Fish. Soc. 74, 310–337. 213.

211. Vishwanath , W, 2010. Schizothorax richardsonii, In : IUCN 2011, IUCN Red list ofThreatened Species Version 2011.2

212. Wada S, Nakamura K, Hatai K: First case of Ochroconis humicola infection in marine culture fish in Japan. Fish Patho130:125-126, 1995

213. Wagner, B. A., Wise, D. J., Khoo, L. H. & Terhune, J. S. 2002 The epidemiology of bacterial disease in food-size channel catfish. J. Aquat. Anim. Health 14, 263–272. (doi:10.1577/ 1548-8667(2002)014,0263:TEOBDI.2.0.CO;2).

214. Walker P.J., Benmansour A., Dietzgen R., Fang R.-X., Jackson A.O., Kurath G., Leong J.C., Nadin-Davies S., Tesh R.B. & Tordo N. (2000) Family Rhabdoviridae. In: Virus Taxonomy. Classification and Nomenclature of Viruses (ed. by M.H.V. Van Regenmortel, C.M. Fauquet, D.H.L. Bishop, E.B. Carstens, M.K. Estes, S.M. Lemon, J. Maniloff, M.A. Mayo, D.J. McGeoch, C.R. Pringle & R.B. Wickner), pp. 563–583. Academic Press, San Diego, CA.

215. Way, K. (1991) Rapid detection of SVC virus antigen in infected cell cultures and clinically diseased carp by enzyme-linked immunosorbent assay (ELISA). Journal of Applied Ichthyology 7, 95–107.

216. Willoughby LG, Roberts RJ (1992) Towards strategic use of fungicides against Saprolegnia parasitica in salmonid fish hatcheries.J Fish Dis 15:1-13,

217. Willoughby LG: Fungi and Fish Diseases, Stirling, Pisces Press, 1994

218. Winfield I.J. (2009) Fish populations. In: Encyclopedia of Inland Waters (Ed. G.E. Likens), pp. 464–472. Elsevier, Oxford, U.K.

219. Wizigmann, G., Pfeil-Putzien, C., Baath, C., Dangschat, H. and Köppel, G. (1980) Serologische Untersuchungen über das Vorkommen von Antikörpern gegenüber Rhabdovirus carpio bei Karpfen in bayerischen Teichwirtschaften. Fisch und Umwelt 8, 30–36.

220. Wolf JC, Smith SA: Systemic zygomycosis in farmed tilapia fish. J Comp Pathol 121:301-306, 1999

221. Wolf K. (1988) Viral hemorrhagic septicemia. In: Fish Viruses and Fish Viral Diseases (ed. by K. Wolf), pp. 217–249.

Comstock Publishing Associates, Cornell University Press, Ithaca and London.

222. Wolke RE: Pathology of bacterial and fungal diseases affecting fish, in Ribelin WE, Migaki G (eds): The Pathology of Fishes. Madison, WI, University of Wisconsin Press, 1975, pp 33-116

223. Yu BH, Kaur R, Lim S, Wang XH, Leung KY. Characterization of extracellular proteins produced by Aeromonas hydrophila AH-1. Proteomics 2007; 7:436-449.

224. Yuasa K, Hati Ira (1995) Relationship between pathogenicity of Saprolegnia spp. isolates to rainbow trout and their biological characteristics. Fish Pathol 30:101-106.

225. Cui, L. C., Guan, X. T., Liu, Z. M., Tian, C. Y., & Xu, Y. G. (2015). Recombinant lactobacillus expressing G protein of spring viremia of carp virus (SVCV) combined with ORF81 protein of koi herpesvirus (KHV): a promising way to induce protective immunity against SVCV and KHV infection in cyprinid fish via oral vaccination. *Vaccine*, *33*(27), 3092-3099.

226. Kanellos, T., Sylvester, I. D., D'Mello, F., Howard, C. R., Mackie, A., Dixon, P. F., ... & Russell, P. H. (2006). DNA vaccination can

protect Cyprinus Carpio against spring viraemia of carp virus. *Vaccine, 24*(23), 4927-4933.

227. Shivappa, R. B., Savan, R., Kono, T., Sakai, M., Emmenegger, E., Kurath, G., & Levine, J. F. (2008). Detection of spring viraemia of carp virus (SVCV) by loop-mediated isothermal amplification (LAMP) in koi carp, Cyprinus carpio L. *Journal of fish diseases, 31*(4), 249-258.

228. Alikin, Y. S., Shchelkunov, I. S., Shchelkunova, T. I., Kupinskaya, O. A., Masycheva, V. I., Klimenko, V. P., & Fadina, V. A. (1996). Prophylactic treatment of viral diseases in fish using native RNA linked to soluble and corpuscular carriers. *Journal of fish biology, 49*(2), 195-205.

229. Siwicki, A. K., Pozet, E., Morand, M., Kazun, B., Trapkowska, S. and Malaczwska, J. (2003): Influence of methisoprinol on the replication of rhabdoviruses isolated from Carp (Cyprinus carpio) and Catfish (Ictalurus melas): in vitro study. Polish Journal of Veterinary Sciences. 6(1):47–50.

WEBSITES LINKS

1. https://en.wikipedia.org/wiki/Dropsy_(fish_disease)

2. http://www.fishhelpline.co.uk/photos/dropsy-01.jpg

3. https://veterinaryresearch.biomedcentral.com/articles/10.1186/1297-9716-44-27/figures/2

4. https://media.springernature.com/lw685/springer-static/image/art%3A10.1186%2F1297-9716-44-27/MediaObjects/13567_2013_Article_234_Fig1_HTML.jpg?as=webp

5. http://2.bp.blogspot.com/_MOTNQWz_Hf0/THLTpu03GUI/AAAAAAAAAOI/rhXetMfebwg/s1600/finrot.jpg\

6. https://fishkeepingguide.net/fin-rot/

7. https://en.bdfish.org/wp-content/uploads/2013/10/epidemic-eye-disease-secondary-stage.jpg

8. https://encrypted-tbn0.gstatic.com/images?q=tbn:ANd9GcRSjdwv2UsQ9-YA1yA7hKjx0pI21bhQN3thxQ&usqp=CAU

9. http://aquafind.com/images/Fungal-Diseases-Of-Fish1.jpg

10. https://ilovepets.co/wp-content/uploads/2015/10/mottled-gills.jpg

11. https://fisheries.tamu.edu/files/2020/01/DSC00938-300x225.jpg

12. https://agritech.tnau.ac.in/fishery/fish_carps_clip_image007.gif

13. http://krishimala.com/sites/default/files/styles/catalogu/public/2018-07/Ichthyophonus%20disease.jpg?itok=0lDY16oo

14. https://prd-wret.s3.us-west-2.amazonaws.com/assets/palladium/production/s3fs-public/styles/full_width/public/thumbnails/image/MMFSDiseaseICHThumb.jpg

15. https://prd-wret.s3.us-west-2.amazonaws.com/assets/palladium/production/s3fs-public/styles/side_image/public/thumbnails/image/HSLDiseaseSVC.jpg

16. https://agritech.tnau.ac.in/fishery/fish_carps_clip_image002_0000.jpg

17. https://en.wikipedia.org/wiki/Viral_hemorrhagic_septicemia

18. https://encrypted-

tbn0.gstatic.com/images?q=tbn:ANd9GcTN
rS-
G7GX8z77e3oNh1ZkaJy5nuKwdjQukkQ
&usqp=CAU